ETC, ETC, ETC…
WISCONSIN VIGNETTES

J.L. Fredrick

Lovstad Publishing
www.Lovstadpublishing.com

ETC, ETC, ETC...

First Edition

Copyright © 2015 Lovstad Publishing
All rights reserved. No part of this book
may be duplicated or transmitted
by any means without written
consent from the publisher.

ISBN: 0692515445
ISBN-13: 978-0692515440

Printed in the United States of America

Research for Chapters 8, 9, & 10 by Ron Nagel
Cover design by Lovstad Publishing
Cover photo by author: View from Brigham Park near
Blue Mounds, WI, looking north toward the Baraboo Range.

OTHER TITLES BY J.L. FREDRICK

Rivers, Roads, & Rails
Ghostville
The Other End of the Tunnel
Aftermath
Cursed by the Wind
Thunder in the Night
Another Shade of Gray
The Gaslight Knights
The Great Train Robbery of Monroe County
September Ten
Mad City Bust
Across the Dead Line
The Private Journal of Clancy Crane
Piano Man
Across the Second Dead Line
Unfinished Business
Dance With a Tornado

CONTENTS

1	Before it was Wisconsin	1
2	The Pineries—Wisconsin Lumber	15
3	Tuesday Morning in Menomonie	31
4	First Brewery in La Crosse	39
5	Appleton Lights	47
6	Taycheedah: Village by the Lake	55
7	Door County Fortress	59
8	Paul Seifert—Folk Artist	65
9	Bogus Bills	69
10	Stanley Edward Lathrop	99
11	Wisconsin Street Cars	115
12	The Clarence Bridge	123
13	Wisconsin Natives	127
14	Shullsburg Under Siege	147

ETC, ETC, ETC…

1

BEFORE IT WAS WISCONSIN

GLACIERS
and
WISCONSIN'S LANDSCAPE

What is now Wisconsin laid beneath the immense weight of a vast sea about 500 million years ago. During that time, Wisconsin history began as the tremendous pressure of the seawater turned the sand to rock—sandstone, to be more precise.

Then, 499 million years later, the ice age began, bringing four monolithic glaciers descending from the northern polar cap, flattening entire mountain ranges, pulverizing them to boulders, pebbles and sand. They carved and scoured the surface, and in some places gouged huge pockets into the earth as they progressed southward. This bulldozing action transformed Wisconsin's mountainous landscape into rolling hills and flatland in comparison to the original terrain, pushing miles and miles of dirt, rock and debris into mounds called a moraine.

Most of Wisconsin lay beneath these massive glaciers. And then, after thousands of years, the temperatures rose and the glaciers receded, ending the ice age. In their wake they deposited boulders, rubble and other debris that had been trapped deep within the miles-thick ice, and the melt water filled the carved pockets and craters forming thousands of lakes and countless acres of marshland that have become integral parts of Wisconsin history.

A very profound aspect of Wisconsin history and its varied landscape occurred in the area that didn't experience glacial coverage. It is called the "driftless area" and includes the western and southwestern portion of the state. This area was merely surrounded by glaciers; it was spared from glacial grinding and pulverization. But the melt water floods created fast-moving rivers that carved their own passages and sculpted some of the most remarkable rock formations in America. Much of the driftless area is rough, rocky terrain, characterized by craggy, elevated cliffs.

It stands to reason, then, that much of the present-day Wisconsin landscape was created by the effects of ice. But that's not all the ice did; it carried with it seeds among all that rubble and debris, deposited them in the soil with the melting, and as temperatures rose, the seeds sprouted and grew, creating a vast area of dense forest and grasslands.

If the ice age was one of the most catastrophic events in the history of this planet, it left behind one of the most incredible landscapes of the modern world.

THE POPULATION EVOLVES

Over 12,000 years ago, just after the glacial ice receded, the first people to live in the area that is now Wisconsin were the Paleo Indians. Hunters and gatherers, they were the first of five culture stages that inhabited the region prior to the arrival of the first European explorers. As the environment changed with the aging of the earth, so did the culture. The next stage—those who lived in the region during the most drastic change—were known as the Archaic Indians, nomadic hunters who fashioned tools from rock.

A more advanced people followed: the Early Woodland culture moved in about 800 B.C. They stored their food supplies, made clay pottery, and buried their dead in mounds. This more sophisticated practice of mound building continued with the Middle and Late Woodland periods, as well. The Late Woodland people created burial mounds in the shapes of animals and birds called effigy mounds that have been discovered throughout southern Wisconsin.

Another cultural group entered Wisconsin during the last few hundred years of the effigy mound era. The Middle Mississippians migrated to Wisconsin from a powerful nation to the south. Their primary city of Cahokia, located across the river from present-day St. Louis, Missouri had a population of some 35,000 people, one of the largest cities in the world at that time. Their uniqueness set them apart from other tribes as they had established trade routes that extended from the Gulf of Mexico to the Great Lakes, and the Atlantic coast to the Rocky Mountains. They settled in two locations in Wisconsin: Aztalan, about mid-way between present-day Madison and Milwaukee along the little Crawfish River; and a city near present-day Trempealeau on the Upper Mississippi River. Both cities were mysteriously abandoned by about 1200 A.D. (You will find more about Aztalan in a later chapter.)

And yet another culture similar to the Mississippians appeared at this time in southern Wisconsin. The Oneota differed from the Mississippians in that they rarely built burial mounds, and they left behind etched pictographic writing on rock walls, indicating that they had advanced to at least a limited written language.

When the first European explorers arrived in Wisconsin, the inhabitants they discovered were the descendants of the Oneota and the Late Woodlanders. The Chippewa were in the north around Lake Superior, the Potawatomi occupied western Wisconsin, and the Menominee, Winnebago, Sauk, Fox and Miami were scattered throughout the entire territory.

All these different tribes practiced farming to some degree, planting crops of corn, squash and beans. Those living in the far north had much shorter growing seasons, so naturally they were more dependent on hunting and fishing for their main source of food. And they all harvested wild rice, nuts, berries, and fruit indigenous to their areas.

As more Europeans immigrated to America, and more of the land on the eastern seaboard was developed and settled, the Native American tribes were pushed farther west. Eventually, Wisconsin inherited some of that population. Among these "refugee" tribes were the Sauk, Mascoutin, Potawatomi, Kickapoo, Ojibwa, Ottawa, and Fox. The influx of these "new" tribes moving into the region did not come without conflict; there were many clashes over territory, and with the introduction of the European fur trade, competition for hunting and trapping grounds caused even more conflict.

EARLY EXPLORERS

Jean Nicolet, a young, adventurous Frenchman came to New France (Canada) in 1618 when Quebec and Montreal were just infant settlements. The governor of New France, Samuel Champlain, recognized in him the qualities of an able ambassador for advancing French interests in the New World, and Nicolet was up to the challenge. He accepted the assignment to a course of training that began with being sent to live among the Indians, to learn their language and customs. After a number of years experiencing many hardships and hunger, he became well-prepared to face the difficulties while engaging a harsh and unfamiliar wilderness as an explorer. He returned to Quebec where he was then employed as a clerk and interpreter for the next two years.

Like many diplomatic leaders of the time, Champlain was eager to discover a short route to India and the Orient; finding it would mean honor and glory for himself and for France.

But it would be a daring mission for any explorer, amidst the warring Indian tribes known to populate the west. Nicolet's first objective was to negotiate peace among the tribes. Then he was to penetrate westward as far as possible in an attempt to discover the passage to China.

With a less-than-accurate map, Nicolet set out westward in a canoe in July, 1634. From Montreal he followed the Ottawa River to Lake Nipissing, then down the French River to Georgian Bay, where he stopped to rest with the Hurons.

His journey continued westward until he reached the Sault Ste. Marie, the waterway connecting Lake Huron and Lake Superior, and then without investigating Lake Superior he turned southward, passing through the Straits of Mackinac. He paddled along the northern shore of Lake Michigan to the mouth of the Menominee River. An Algonquin tribe there told him about "Men of the Sea" not far distant. Nicolet jumped to the conclusion that he had almost reached China.

Donned in an elegant Oriental robe, he pressed on to the head of the bay, intending to impress the people of

China. When he arrived, however, he was met by a band of Winnebago Indians whose language he didn't understand. Greatly disappointed—and perhaps embarrassed—that he had not discovered the China shore, Nicolet proceeded, though, to negotiate a peace agreement between the Winnebago and Huron tribes, and urged them to transport their furs to Montreal to trade for the white man's goods. The negotiations were a success, and the occasion was celebrated with a great feast of wild game.

Nicolet continued his expedition southward on the Fox River to Lake Winnebago, and then on to a Mascoutin Indian village at approximately the site of present-day Berlin in Green Lake County. Although he heard this tribe talk about the Mississippi River, he failed to recognize its importance.

Instead of continuing his journey westward, he chose to travel south where he visited with the Illinois tribes, and then returned to the Fox River and Green Bay.

About one year after he had begun, Nicolet returned to Montreal in July 1635 without ever seeing the Mighty Mississippi River.

Twenty years later, two more Frenchmen arrived in the Green Bay territory. Pierre Radisson and Menard Groseilliers remained for two years. They, too, visited with several native tribes—the Ottawa, Mascoutin, and Pottawatomi—but they went no farther west than Nicolet had been. It is likely that their intensions were not necessarily focused on exploration, but rather to establish trading relation with the natives, as in 1659 they started out on another voyage that followed Nicolet's earlier route to Sault Ste. Marie, and then westward to Lake Superior, where, on Chequamegon Bay they built a small fort and entered into friendly relations with the Hurons.

Radisson and Groseilliers joined the Hurons for the winter hunt, however, deep snow and harsh weather prevented much success, and a period of famine resulted in 500 or more deaths from starvation among the natives. The two French voyagers narrowly escaped the same fate, managing to survive by eating tree bark until the weather allowed them to attain a small supply of game. Further wanderings took them into Sioux country across the St. Croix River.

The governor of New France (Canada) was not in favor of their expedition, and when they returned to Montreal in August 1660, their more than 300 beaver pelts were confiscated. Naturally, they were so angered by this, that they offered their services to the English. Eventually, King Charles II granted a charter for the Hudson Bay Fur Company, and the French lost the splendid fur trade of a vast region.

The French, however, continued to apply their influence in the land that would become Wisconsin. To further their relations with the natives, missionaries were sent to convert the Indians to peaceful, God-fearing people. Father Rene Menard, a Jesuit, came with a returning party of trading Indians in 1660. They abandoned him on the shores of

Keweenaw Bay, and after a deplorable winter, with only one companion he started out to re-join the Huron fugitives, former members of the Ontario mission; they were thought to be occupying the region that was the headwaters of the Black River. During his journey down the Wisconsin River in a small craft, Father Menard was lost at one of the upper river portages. Whether he was killed by beast or native is not absolutely certain, but because his cassock and kettle were later found in a Sioux lodge, it is likely that he was murdered.

Five years later, Father Claude Allouez was sent to continue the work of Father Menard. Although he suffered many hardships in his efforts, he was a man of determination. At Chequamegon Bay—near the present city of Ashland—he constructed a rudimentary chapel, the first Christian church erected in Wisconsin, and for two years he taught religion to natives from the entire Wisconsin territory. Then in 1669 he moved to the area of Green Bay. There he established missions along the bay shore, and in the Fox and Wolf River valleys among the Menominee, Pottawatomi, Sauk, Fox, Miami, Mascoutin, and Kickapoo native tribes. Father Allouez and his fellow workers built the first permanent Wisconsin mission—At. Francis Xavier established in 1671—at the DePere rapids on the Fox River.

That same year, the king of France, Louis XIV, declared possession of all this western country for the French sovereignty. He enlisted Nicholas Perrot, a notable fur trader and explorer of the territory since 1665, to assemble the chiefs of the Wisconsin native tribes to attend a ceremony on the western shore of Sault Ste. Marie, in recognition of this great occasion. They watched in awe as priests and warriors chanted praise of God and of the French King, and made the declaration that all the Indians' country west of Lake Michigan was annexed to the French domain, and that all natives of this land were, from that day forward, subjects of a foreign monarch.

The French leader sent yet another pair of explorers on an expedition to seek a water passage route to the Orient. It was still unknown that a vast continent stretched 2,000 miles before them. Father Jacques Marquette (a Jesuit Priest) and Louis Jolliet, (priest turned fur trader) reached the Mississippi via the Fox River, Lake Winnebago, and the Wisconsin River by June 1673, making them the first to navigate the full distance of the Wisconsin. Their journey provided the first official information about the entire territory, and marked the beginning of French control of the land that remained until the end of the French and Indian War in 1763.

A few years later, Nicholas Perrot was installed as Governor-General of the new French territory west of Lake Michigan. He established a number of trading posts, most of them along the Upper Mississippi River. It was at Fort St. Antoine on the east bank of Lake Pepin in 1689 that Perrot declared for France the possession of the Sioux territory, and he was the first European to discover and explore the lead mine region of southwestern Wisconsin.

Little was known about the Wisconsin territory by the people of the English colonies on the Atlantic coast, or by anyone except the French until 1778 when Capt. Jonathan Carver of Connecticut published his book of travels through the region, which he had done twelve years before. He had visited the Green Bay settlement (then called Fort Edward Augustus, where there were a few French families) and then went on to visit a large Winnebago community at the entrance of Lake Winnebago. His travels took him to Prairie du Chien via the Fox and Wisconsin Rivers, stopping along the way at a village of the Sacs near the site of present-day Prairie du Sac, and at a village of Fox near present-day Muscoda. From Prairie du Chien, his expedition continued up the Mississippi to Lake Pepin. During his exploration in what would become Minnesota, he spent several months among the Sioux, and after his return to civilization, he claimed that he had been given a grant by the Sioux of some 14,000 square miles of lands in the Mississippi River Valley. In later years, his descendants attempted to establish claims on that land, however, the claims were denied by Congress.

THE FUR TRADING ERA

Fur pelts from deer, elk, bear, and especially beaver were in high demand in Europe, and the French had cornered the market with their new-found source in the land of Wisconsin with its numerous lakes, rivers, and eager cooperation of the Native American hunters and trappers.

But the British had muscled their way into the fur trade, and conflicts erupted over the control of the land as well as the fur trade. After years of conflicts that culminated in the French and Indian War, the British finally won. The Treaty of Paris ceded all of Canada and the land that France claimed along the Mississippi River to the British, and they relinquished their fur trading empire as well.

The French fur trade had introduced the first European influence to Wisconsin, and as the British gained control, not much changed. The region remained sparsely settled, except for the Native Americans and the traders. Few Europeans wanted to settle in the midst of harsh winters and frequent Indian conflicts. But many of the traders actually lived with the Indians and took Indian wives. It was a dangerous lifestyle if they attempted to settle on their own, as there was yet no government or any form of protection from Indian uprisings.

The British did make some changes to the fur trade, however. Furs were now sent to London instead of Paris. British investors brought about the increase in size of the trading companies and spread them farther into the northwest as the beaver population dwindled. This growth of large trade companies reduced the power of the Native tribes. The British managed to maintain control of the fur trade after the American Revolution, but then they were finally forced out after the War of 1812.

By the time Americans had complete control of the

trade, it was unfortunately in serious decline. Tremendous reduction of the beaver population and the removal of the Native Americans to reservations combined to devastate the fur trade in the Wisconsin Territory. Traders were now moving their operations to the untouched Pacific Northwest where fur-bearing wildlife was still bountiful. Wisconsin had served as successful trading headquarters for the French, British, and Americans for nearly 200 years, but now the decline in the fur trade allowed the territory to shift from a frontier wilderness to a settled civilization.

THE AMERICAN REVOLUTION and the WAR OF 1812

Not many Americans lived in the Wisconsin region, nor was Wisconsin a part of the United States at the time of the American Revolution, so it was little affected by the war. American victory did little to change the area; French and British traders still remained scattered throughout the region, and even though all the trading posts were in American hands twenty years later, the British still continued to control the trade from Canada.

Only after another war with England, the War of 1812, did the Americans take control of the fur trade. Following the American victory, the American flag was finally raised on Wisconsin soil, and the Wisconsin Territory was officially part of the United States.

2

THE PINERIES—WISCONSIN LUMBER

When the American frontier began to push westward beyond the Appalachian Mountains, to the prairies of northern Indiana and Illinois, and then to the vast plains across the Mississippi, the pioneers were faced with a problem they had never experienced before—lack of building materials. Where they came from in the east, there had always been an abundant wood supply. But on the treeless plains of the west, they were forced to turn to alternate construction methods. Absence of timber meant fewer difficulties in creating clear farm land, but how and with what to build homes, barns and fences became a challenge. One solution was to make use of the sod that covered the prairies; this plentiful material sufficed for a time, but to satisfy the desire for structures of a more permanent nature, something better was needed. The only option was to transport good building materials from the nearest source.

The abundant forests of the Great Lakes region provided the best answer. Woodland extending westward from the New England states covered northern Michigan, Wisconsin and Minnesota with a seemingly inexhaustible supply of desirable pine timber, a wealth that far surpassed any world treasure.

The heavily-forested lands of Wisconsin were primarily the northern two-thirds of the state, comprised of a thirty to fifty-mile-wide band of hardwoods at the southern edge, then mixed hardwoods and conifers, and surrounding the headwaters of the St. Croix, Chippewa, Black, Wisconsin, Menominee and Wolf Rivers, pine was the predominant species.

White pine lumber was the preferred building material, as it was light-weight and easily workable. But equally important, its buoyancy made it ideal to transport by floating on the waterways, whereas the dense, heavier hardwoods tended to sink to the bottom of the rivers.

Northern Wisconsin held the ideal conditions for pine timber, and the lumber industry; the glaciers that once covered most of the region not only pulverized rocky terrain to a sandy soil perfect for the pine forest growth, but they carved out the many riverbeds that provided the all-important means of transporting the logs to the sawmills. Long before any railroads were built into the forest regions, the rivers were most useful to the lumber industry. During the spring, as a result of the melting heavy snowfalls all winter, the high, fast-moving currents of the rivers provided a powerful energy to send the millions of logs downstream to be distributed to the many mills for processing into useable lumber. They flowed to th Great Lakes, and mostly to the Mississippi River, the waterway that was most instrumental in the building of the American West. Wisconsin lumber was even freighted to the eastern markets, as well, until commercial lumbering began in the Virginias.

Even though the virgin pine forests were there, and the rivers were there, logging and lumbering in Wisconsin wasn't an active industry until the 1840s. fur trading and lead mining were still the primary sources of economic wealth. Lead miners in southwestern Wisconsin and northwestern Illinois who chose to remain through the winter months had no materials to construct suitable homes, so they were obliged to burrow caves into the hills for shelter, hence, gaining them the nickname "Badgers," a pseudonym that has remained popular among Wisconsinites to present day. When the first territorial capital building was to be erected at Belmont in 1836, there was no readily available lumber, so the necessary materials had to be shipped from Pennsylvania down the Ohio River, up the Mississippi to Galena, and then overland 25 miles by ox teams and wagons to the site of the new capitol. The scarcity of lumber held its price at a premium, and in many cases it was less expensive to have a house constructed in Pennsylvania and then transport it in sections by riverboat to Wisconsin.

Why, then, was the production of lumber so greatly delayed when there was so much available timber and even a viable means to transport it? There are a number of reasonable explanations.

Until the US Government negotiated legal possession of the land, the northern timberland rightfully belonged to the natives. It was unlawful for anyone to enter into logging operations on any Indian lands without special permission. Ironically, the government took what it needed to build military installations at Green Bay, Portage, and Prairie du Chien long before legal title was obtained, recognizing the difficulty in justifying prosecution of others cutting what they wanted. For example, in 1828 at the portage between the Fox and Wisconsin Rivers where Fort Winnebago was to be established (present-day site of Portage, Wisconsin), Second Lieutenant Jefferson Davis led a company of soldiers up the Wisconsin River to a fine tract of pine timber. They cut logs and floated them downriver to the portage where they were carted the rest of the way to the building site. There, the logs were cut into lumber with hand tools. Within two years, enough timber was cut to construct seven barracks buildings, two blockhouses, and outside of the fort proper, wash houses, commissary store, icehouse, blacksmith shop, carpenter shop, bakeshop, and stables.

Regardless of the risks of being charged with trespassing, some small scale loggers didn't wait for the land to be surveyed and sold by the government, or for the legal formalities to allow them use of the public domain. The War Department did issue permits to log on Indian land after

1830, even though the Secretary of War had no statutory right to issue such documents. These permits didn't protect the bearer from the risks, but merely assured them that the War Department wouldn't interfere with reasonable logging operations.

Another reason for the lumber industry delay in Wisconsin was the lack of investment capital. Money was in short supply in the west, and the capitalists and businessmen of the east weren't interested in pursuing such endeavors as long as the forest lands still belonged to the natives. And without the migration of skilled labor in adequate numbers, the development of the industry would have to wait for treaties to be signed.

With or without permits, sporadic logging operations were conducted in Wisconsin as early as 1810 in the areas of Green Bay, the Black River, the Chippewa River, and the Wisconsin River. These early loggers could hardly be credited with the founding of the industry, as their work wasn't of a permanent nature. But they did, however, blaze the trail to commercial lumbering for those who followed.

By 1830, immigration began to push settlers into Indian country in relatively large numbers. But the federal government had, so far, failed to remove the Indians by acquiring the pine forest lands of the Great Lakes region. Lack of sufficient building materials was hindering progress in the southern areas, as well. Then in 1832 a band of Sauk and Fox led by Chief Black Hawk threatened the rising population, resulting in the dreary event known as the Black Hawk War. Pillaging and murdering on their path northward out of Illinois into Wisconsin, they were met by the much stronger US Militia, and were soon on the run, this time in a survival attempt. The Indians were defeated in a relatively short time, and the government began negotiating treaties that provided "reservation" areas in Wisconsin, and relocated many to areas west of the Mississippi River.

The treaties that, for the most part, resolved the Indian issues produced a rush of immigrants to Wisconsin. Eastern businessmen aware of the large profits in the lumber industry of New York considered the Wisconsin woodlands a good investment. Nearly 900,000 acres of land had been purchased by settlers and speculators by the end of 1836. Excitement over this newly opened region became so great that corner building lots in some villages were selling—sight unseen—for as much as $15,000 to buyers in New York.

Despite the economic panic of 1837 that brought land speculation to an abrupt halt, the lumber industry continued to grow; it had not yet begun to meet the demand for building materials in the Mississippi Valley. Entrepreneurs who had scouted the region for tracts of timberland associated themselves with capitalists, and soon returned to the wilderness to build mills and homes and other facilities necessary to their enterprise. Most of them raised vegetables and grains for their own food and for their cattle. Before the land had been surveyed and put up for sale, a dozen or more companies were established in the territory ceded by the Winnebago and the Chippewa, and many more were forthcoming. Their shortcoming was, however, that the founders of these operations knew very little about the techniques required for running a lumbering business in the wilderness, and were quite handicapped for the lack of workers experienced in logging, manufacturing, and transporting their product. Consequently, it became necessary to import skilled managers and laborers from the older lumber communities of New Brunswick, Maine, New Hampshire, New York, and Pennsylvania. The men starting out in this new industry attracted skilled lumbermen by purchasing advertising space in New England newspapers and sent large amounts of promotional literature describing the prosperous possibilities of lumbering in the new territory, and the vast quantity of government timberland available for a nominal price. The papers informed eastern readers of the high wages paid to skilled workers, cheap lumber for building homes, prosperity to farmers who would supply the lumbermen with produce, and the success of those who had already arrived. This advertising combined with the gradual decline of lumber production in the eastern areas proved quite successful in luring skilled lumbermen to the Wisconsin pineries; they came by the hundreds. After 1840, many more came from Scandinavian countries, Germany, and Ireland. During the next fifteen years the population in the logging areas more than doubled.

Not only did this advertising attract a work force, but it also attracted numerous lumber barons from the east— men who had money to invest and to establish companies that employed the growing work force. The legislature of Wisconsin sweetened the deal by setting the legal interest rate at twelve percent. Wisconsin offered opportunities unknown in any other state in the Union.

With the great opportunities came immense difficulties, as well. It should not be surprising that more lumbering operations failed than succeeded. The task of merely penetrating into the wilderness and overcoming the seemingly insurmountable obstacles for rather meager initial earnings was discouraging. Creating a business so far removed from civilization created the problems of transporting supplies and equipment to the lumbermen. Few farmers had yet settled to produce food for the logging and mill crews; such supplies, as well as necessities like clothing, dry goods, ironwork, mill machinery and tools had to be carried by keel boats and teams over extremely difficult routes. The high transportation costs defeated many operations.

It was for this reason that some enterprising lumbermen met the problem by starting their own freighting and store business. For example, an Eau Claire logging and mill operation, Ingram, Kennedy and Company, also became a large freighting business using a custom-built steamboat that ran the Chippewa River between Read's Landing on the Mississippi and Eau Claire.

The early mills and dams were subject to nature's perils, too. Construction quality had not yet advanced, and floods often swept away everything—mill, dam, and an entire supply of logs. Adversely, low water levels due to less-than-normal snowfall during the winter meant fewer logs arriving at the mills. And fire was always an ongoing threat.

When a mill had conquered all the inherent mechanical and natural dangers of the industry, it still faced the possibility of a financial panic, as happened in 1857, and again in 1873. Markets filled to capacity as supply exceeded the demand, and lumber prices plummeted to a catastrophic level.

Despite all the pitfalls, nothing could prevent the constant growth of lumber manufacturing in Wisconsin. By 1845 it completely overshadowed fur trading and mining, and it had created a demand for agricultural products, significantly increasing the rise in that industry, as well. Lumbering in Wisconsin had unquestionably become big business when, in 1872, mills in the state produced well over a billion board feet of lumber, not including minor products such as lath and shingles. Eastern manufacturers could no longer compete with the production in Wisconsin; the market had permanently changed. Wisconsin pineries were in control of supplying building materials to the Mississippi Valley and the West.

Western expansion after the Civil War and the rapid

advancement of the railroad network gave the Great Lakes region lumber trade its final and lasting boost. Speedier delivery to a nation-wide market left lumbermen only imagining what their industry would become.

LUMBER WAR

As the lumber industry expanded in Wisconsin there arose within it two conflicting interests that contributed a new chapter to the industrial history of the state. On one hand were arrayed the sawmill interests within the pineries, whose ambition was to manufacture into lumber, without interference, all the pine that was cut from the Wisconsin forests; on the other were the log driving interests whose function it was to supply raw material to the immense mills that lined the Mississippi River and the shores of Green Bay and Lake Winnebago. Nearly every important pinery stream in the state faced this conflict of interests during the period from 1857 to 1873, and the deciding clash in each case came during the decade of the sixties.

Prior to 1860 this question was nowhere regarded as important. Nearly all the logs cut in the northern forests of Wisconsin were manufactured into lumber within the pineries themselves. Perhaps a third of the small annual cut of the St. Croix and the Black was driven down the Mississippi River to supply the sawmills along its banks in Wisconsin, Iowa and Illinois. On the Chippewa River the quantity of pine disposed of in that manner was negligible; on the Wisconsin there was practically none. During the closing years of the Civil War, however, the Mississippi River mills began to lay heavier impact upon the Wisconsin forests. The alarmed sawmill owners of Wisconsin found as a result that they were obliged to pay higher prices for logs. Even more disquieting was the fact that dangerous sawmill competitors were securing a foothold in the very heart of their markets. On the Chippewa, Black and St. Croix, log driving for lower mills consumed particularly menacing proportions, and upon those streams, resulting controversies were correspondingly sharp.

The most spectacular clash occurred upon the Chippewa River, and is known as the *Beef Slough War*. This may be described in some detail, for not only was it typical of the others, but it was representative also of the standard of business ethics of the time. It foreshadowed, moreover, new developments in the lumber industry of the northwest. Out of it there arose the great lumber syndicate of its day, an organization that constituted the beginning of what became the strongest lumber power on the North American continent.

It so happened that the Chippewa River, near its mouth, divides into two channels, one of which is, for the most part, not navigable and is commonly known as Beef Slough. Beef Slough at that time formed an admirable harbor for the sorting and rafting of logs to be taken down the Mississippi River. The mill men of the Chippewa River were aware of this fact and near the close of the Civil War set about forestalling its use in any such capacity. They purchased the land at its entrance and in 1866 secured from the legislature special logging privileges there, which they had no intention of using, but only holding against possible future users.

Early in 1867 another association, consisting of prominent loggers of Michigan, Fond du Lac and Oshkosh, who had interests in the sawmills on the Mississippi River, organized a log driving association known as the *Beef Slough Manufacturing, Booming, Log Driving and Transportation Company,* and applied to the legislature for a charter to erect within Beef Slough the booms and piers necessary for their work. The bill was defeated, and immediately the victorious mill men of Eau Claire and Menomonie sent a crew of some hundreds of their employees with rafts of slabs up the entrance to the menacing slough. The logging company promptly swore out an injunction against the mill men, but not soon enough to prevent the completion of the dam. The next step that it took was more effective, however. Shrewdly dispossessing the mill men of their ownership of the head of the slough by prevailing upon friendly local authorities to condemn the land for a public highway, they forcibly tore out the offending obstruction. The latter undertaking threatened for a time to lead to a pitched battle between the opposing sawmill and the driving factions, but fortunately resulted only in a words war in rivermen's English.

Such was the status of the controversy when the legislature of 1869 convened. The logging company again made an effort to secure a charter, but its bill was decisively defeated in the assembly near the close of the session. A few days after the vote, however, an innocent appearing measure was introduced in the senate providing for the incorporation of the Portage City Gas Light Company. It was less than a week before adjournment. The bill was pushed through the legislature with the rush of business that was always present at the close of sessions, and was signed by the governor a few hours before the appointed time for adjournment.

Several days after the Portage City bill had thus become law it was learned that hidden away near its close was the following provision: "In all cases where any franchise or privilege has been or shall be granted by law to several persons, the grant shall be deemed several as well as joint, so that one or more may accept and exercise the franchise alone." The logging company had won its fight, for one of its members was a mill man who in 1866 had been associated with the Chippewa mill men as an incorporator in their unused charter. It was but a matter of form for him to assign to his new associates the rights and privileges that the secret joker in the Portage City bill had given him. The public chuckled over the sly maneuver, while the two opponents prepared for a renewal of hostilities.

Within a few months the season for the log drive from the pineries was at hand. The logging company served notice upon the mill men along the Chippewa to pass unmolested all logs bearing the Beef Slough mark. The sawmill owners were not only unwilling, but unable to do this, for only two of them possessed the necessary sorting facilities. Moreover, they were unwilling to agree upon a system of log exchanges such as had governed operations on the river until that time. Here was a deadlock, in which force again proved to be the only arbiter. The Beef Slough log drivers, numbering seventy-five rough, belligerent fellows, on their way down from the pineries were not shy to cut open whatever sawmill reservoirs they found containing any of their logs, taking from these not only their own logs but large quantities of others.

In Eau Claire County there awaited them the opposing army of the sawmill owners, numbering some 200 equally rough and determined men led by the county sheriff. As the two forces approached, the excitement and danger of a bloody clash increased. Fortunately, however, an open battle was averted. The sawmill army was too overwhelming to be resisted, and the leaders of the drive were obliged to submit to arrest. A settlement and an armed truce were eventually effected and the drivers continued on their way.

For several years after 1868, the disputes and contentions of the log driving and sawmill interests of the Chippewa River continued. In 1870 the Beef Slough Company secured from the legislature a confirmation and extension of its charter, but by this time its stormy life had brought it to bankruptcy. Its improvements were leased at the close of 1870 to an association of Mississippi River sawmill owners, among whom the leading spirit was Frederick Weyerhaeuser, the future lumber king of America. Early in 1871 this association organized the Mississippi River Logging Company, which soon became the greatest lumber syndicate of its time.

3

TUESDAY MORNING IN MENOMONIE

Tuesday morning, October 20, 1931, in Menomonie, Wisconsin appeared to be, for the most part, just like any other weekday; the activity of four men, however, would prove it to be far from a normal day of business.

Minneapolis/St. Paul, Minnesota had become a harbor for gangsters and hoodlums, the likes of which equaled those found in Chicago, Kansas City, and other dens of crime around the country. One of them was Frank Keating, originally from Chicago. In February of the previous year, Keating and another hoodlum named Charles Harmon had taken an unauthorized departure from Leavenworth Prison, walking casually out the prison gates using a couple of trustee passes. Keaton had gotten twenty-five years' hard time for a robbery gone bad—a heist of the US Mail of $135,000—that only got him a long time to think about what had gone wrong. (The story goes that the stolen passes were given to them by bank robber George Kelly, better known to the public as "Machine Gun Kelly.)

Once successfully out of confinement, they headed to the Twin Cities where they would associate and work at one time or another with other famous names in felony such as Alvin "Creepy" Karpis; Freddie Barker, vile son of the outrageous Ma Barker; and none other than Frank "Jelly" Nash who was later killed during the famed Kansas City Massacre, in which several law officers also died.

In those wild times, a fully automatic weapon could be purchased without the complex licensing and background checks required now. The cost of a Thompson submachine gun was about $250 by mail order, and it quickly became the favorite firepower of robber gangs because of its high volume of fire and its power of intimidation. Keating and his buddies liked the Thompson, too, and had one with them on October 20, 1931 when they went to raid the Kraft State Bank in Menomonie. They chose the morning hours, certain that the bank's vault would be open for their withdrawal request.

Keating and his three associates, Frank Webber, Tommy Holden, and Charles Harmon, cruised into Menomonie in a big, black Lincoln. (Bandits in those days liked big cars with lots of horsepower.) They parked in the 400 block of Main Street, ironically right in front of Frank Hintzman's Emporium that offered not only new furniture, but also funeral arrangements for the dearly departed.

In true gangster fashion, driver Frank Webber stayed with the car and kept the motor running. He, too, was a convicted bank robber who had done time in Salt Lake City, and was appropriately described by the *Minneapolis Star* as "a notorious police character."

At 9:15 a.m. with Webber waiting and ready to whisk away the others as they fled the bank with the loot, Keating, Holden, and Harmon walked down Main Street with their concealed weapons about a half block to the Kraft State Bank. The bank had just opened its doors for the beginning of the day's business. A few patrons were already being served at the teller counters by the bank staff: President William Kraft; his sons, James and William; daughter Vera; cousin Ruby Kraft; teller Mrs. A. Schaefer; another assistant cashier Hendrickson; and bank stenographer Madelyn Gullickson.

The hold-up went smoothly at first. The bandits ordered the bank employees and patrons to lie on the floor, and when they had quickly stripped the tellers' drawers of ready cash, they turned on the bank's president, William Kraft, and announced, "We want the rest of the money."

"Sorry," Kraft said. "You've got all there is."

The robbers weren't satisfied with the response and weren't about to be deterred so easily. One of them shot nineteen-year-old son James, an assistant cashier, in the shoulder and continued to demand more money. Another outlaw, convinced that Kraft was lying, and extremely aggravated by the refusal to produce more cash, shot the other son, William, twice as he lay helplessly on the floor. (Later reported in "grave" condition, William would survive.)

About that time, an alert bank security officer tripped the bank's alarm. It was loud enough for Webber to hear a half block away; he reacted immediately. Pulling the Lincoln away from the curb, he stopped in the middle of the street in front of the bank and jumped out with his Thompson submachine gun. He opened both left doors, stood between them and fired periodic bursts down the street to discourage anybody to come to the aid of the bank men.

The roar of the robbers' .45s inside the confines of the bank combined with the racket of the Tommy gun out in the street, there could be no doubt that everybody in town had to know there was trouble at the bank. Money or no money, Keaton and his two assistants knew it was time to clear the bank, and the town, as rapidly as possible. They grabbed Kraft's wounded son, James, and teller Mrs. Schaefer as shields, pushed them out the bank doors and then headed for Webber and the waiting getaway car.

A large crowd of angry citizens had already gathered outside. In the confusion, Mrs. Schaefer stumbled and fell. As the bandits ran to the waiting car, she managed to escape to shelter, but young James, badly injured, was unable to run. He remained a hostage as they hustled into the car and drove off at a high rate of speed.

Vernon Townsend, the bank guard who had sounded the alarm, was under strict instructions not to fire his weapon among patrons inside the bank, but he had managed to leave his special observation post above the tellers' cages and dashed to the roof where he opened fire on the getaway car, hitting the gas tank and possibly one of the robbers as well.

By this time some of the citizens had found weapons and began firing at the fleeing vehicle. Winfield Kern, the owner of a nearby restaurant, fired shots through his own plate-glass window. Ed Grudt started shooting from a second story window in the Farmer Store building. Return fire from Webber's Tommy gun busted window framing and shattered glass, but missed Grudt. Ed Kinkle's rounds penetrated the rear window of the Lincoln sedan, and he said later that he had heard somebody inside the car yell as his bullets struck the car. It was learned later that Kinkle's bullets did hit the Lincoln, and it was probably his shot that struck Webber's eye, a painful wound that would later prove fatal.

Under-Sheriff Jack Harmon reported a further gunfight on the road a short distance from Menomonie, and it could have been during this exchange that Webber was hit. Newspaper reports stated that Harmon had "unloaded a round at the car," and that "simultaneously one of the fugitives slumped in his seat." Another paper added that when last seen, "the driver was bleeding profusely at the mouth and some who saw the car claimed that one of the other two in the car was wrapped in a blanket as if he, too, had been wounded."

The big Lincoln roared away from town, racing east on Hwy 12, then turning off onto County Road B. As they fled, the outlaws pitched handfuls of nails onto the roadway, hopeful of flattening the tires of any pursuing automobiles.

An armed posse in a number of cars streamed out of town in hot pursuit; they found Webber's corpse along the road about eight miles out. The Dunn County News reported that the outlaw's "right eye and temple were torn by a bullet. The bandit wore a steel vest and carried two revolvers. The fleeing bandits also threw out a loose steel vest when they hurled their dead accomplice onto the road."

Tragically, a man hauling milk found young Kraft's body, shot in the back of the head and dumped in a roadside ditch, perhaps in revenge for the killing of Webber. Sheriff Ike Harmon and a steadily growing posse continued the search for the outlaws, but with no success.

When people of the area heard about Kraft's murder, hundreds of citizens from six counties joined police officers in the hunt. An airplane was pressed into service for the search, but its pilot found nothing.

A woman who had joined the hunt some miles north of Menomonie spotted a car stopped alongside the road; its windows were shot out, and two of the occupants were bandaging a third man. But the amateur first aid had accomplished little, for Charles Harmon's body was found a little later beside the road at Shell Lake. It was unknown who fired the shots that caused his wounds, but before he died, the other bandits had stopped the car, found a place to lay Harmon on the ground, then left him with bandages and iodine and a handful of the bank loot in case he survived his wounds. But he didn't survive.

Also found were some of the bandits' weaponry—the submachine gun and two hand guns. Frank Keating and Tommy Holden were gone; they had somehow found a successful escape route.

Charles Harmon was positively identified as one of the bank robbers by Ruby Kraft. He was also identified in connection with two other bank robberies that had recently occurred in Duluth and Colfax. Harmon was a Texan with a long history of crime; he had spent jail time in his home state, as well as at Leavenworth, Kansas where he had eventually partnered with Keating.

Finally, searchers discovered the bandits' getaway car, abandoned and burned about six miles east of Webster. The rear window had been shot out and the back seat was soaked with blood. There was no sign of the fleeing outlaws, but a farmer had witnesses the two men setting fire to the Lincoln, and then sped away in another car that was apparently waiting to take them farther.

The two remaining holdup men were reported to be seen sometime later in northern Minnesota, but then they disappeared altogether. Searchers questioned an assortment of possible accomplices and even inquired at hospitals hoping to turn up anyone who might have been treated for suspicious gunshot wounds. Several suspects were arrested, but lack of evidence—or proof of innocence—set them free.

One arrest, however, did lead to a trial. Robert Newbern had been acquitted of an earlier bank robbery and murder in Minneapolis, so he appeared to be a likely participant at the Menomonie holdup. But he won an acquittal there, too.

The two dead robbers spent some time on public display at a local funeral parlor where crowds of citizens viewed them, but nobody claimed the remains. Two weeks after the robbery, the bodies were taken to Potter's Field where they were buried in a single grave.

Keating and Holden had learned nothing from their narrow escape at Menomonie. They recruited more low life and continued to rob more banks in various towns of Minnesota. But their days were numbered. In less than a year, federal agents located them and laid a trap.

Their capture, however, was nothing as spectacular as that of John Dillinger or Pretty Boy Floyd. In the summer of 1932, FBI agents easily collared them and another outlaw on the Old Mission Golf Course in Kansas City. It was rumored that "Jelly" Nash was there too, but because he was such a lousy golfer, he was off in the farthest reaches of the rough and managed to escape arrest.

Keating and Holden were sentenced to life in prison; they both died there.

4

FIRST BREWERY IN LA CROSSE

The rise of the brewing industry in La Crosse, Wisconsin pre-dates the Civil War and Victorian periods in the history of the city. It developed into what became one of the city's leading industries.

John Gund Sr. came to La Crosse in 1854, just thirteen years after Nathan Myrick first settled on Barron's Island. (Pettibone) He found La Crosse to be not much more than a trading post. But settlers were pouring in into this new territory every month. With the prospect of a growing population, Gund took up one of his two trades that he knew best—brewing.

Gund was born October 3, 1830 at Schwetzingen, a small village in Germany. His father, George Gund, was a hop and tobacco farmer. John learned two trades—cooperage and brewing. After his parents left for United States in 1847 he continued working in Germany for a year. At the age of 18 he sailed for New York, and then traveled to Freeport, Illinois where his parents had located.

From Freeport he went to Galena, Illinois, and then to

Dubuque, Iowa where he worked in the brewery there, but he soon returned to Galena to become involved with the operations of two breweries. Four years later he went to La Crosse and built his own brewery.

That first brewery was housed in a small log building on the southeast corner of what is now Front and Division Streets. Mr. Gund believed that a brewery should be located at the edge of the city, and outside the city limits. He chose that location because, at the time, La Crosse was comprised of only a handful of structures. For the same reason, in later years, he erected is new plant on the prairie land that is now along South Avenue.

Gund's first year of business in La Crosse was on a very small scale compared to the production of his Empire Brewery a half-century later. In that first year his output was 500 barrels of beer, with only a dozen men working for him. Fifty years later, his Empire Brewery employed several hundred.

For four long years Gund worked at his trade in his own brewery, but in 1858 he went into partnership with Gottlieb Heileman, building and opening the City Brewery, later to be known as the G. Heileman Brewery.

But Gund was not without competition; another brewer, Frederick Defengaber, made a bold effort to establish his business in 1856. But the antiquated machinery used in that brewery was never upgraded, and prevented any progress. History records that Defengaber left the city in 1870. Two years after the competing brewery had closed,

John Gund branched out; in 1872 he dissolved partnership with Mr. Heileman and built the Empire Brewery on South Avenue.

Also, about 1856, a Dr. Nicolai began brewing beer in a small building at what is now Second and Pearl Streets. A year later, Charles and John Michel opened the first brewery of any size in La Crosse at Third and Division Streets; their first year of business yielded 1,000 barrels of lager beer.

In those early days the method and process of brewing was naturally crude and uncultured as compared with the scientific art of brewing as it was eventually mastered. At that time, the workmen usually had their sleeping quarters in the brewery, working twelve- eighteen-hour days. All work was done by hand, the operations being naturally slow and tedious. For instance, the cleansing of kegs and bottles was done in a most primitive manner. Pitch heated to a liquid form was poured into a keg and the keg was then rolled back and forth. In later years the kegs were cleansed, inspected, pre-heated, and pitched in one operation by means of more modern machinery.

When brewers began to produce bottled beer, a small quantity of lead shot was placed in each bottle, which was shaken by hand for the purpose of loosening any particles of dirt in the bottle. Subsequently they were rinsed out in water in the same crude way. Each bottle was handled separately in this process of cleaning, pasteurizing, and labeling. With "modern" equipment the bottles were placed in a soaker machine, automatically passing through a caustic solution and on to the automatic brushing machine. Later they went through the pasteurizer. Labeling machines attached the gummed paper labels to the bottles.

Refrigeration was not known in those early days, yet the beer had to be dept cool. As a consequence, the beer was made in the winter months and hauled by sleighs to the bluffs along the Mormon Coulee Road where large caves had been dug into the cliffs. The beer was pumped from the kegs into large wooden tanks in the caves; there the beer was stored and retrieved as needed during the summer. Many a story was told of the days when large bobsleds carted great loads of beer kegs to these caves, overturning on the way, sending the full kegs rolling merrily down the hillside.

At the time the Civil War began, there were just four breweries in operation in La Crosse. In most cases, they were but humble beginnings of what in later years were to develop into a great industry. The Civil War years saw little progress, but during the reconstruction period that followed, the brewing business again began to boom. New breweries opened and the older firms started to expand. However, many of the smaller firms did not survive the last half of the Nineteenth Century.

The period from the Civil War to 1890 was most important in the development of the industry, however, not until the advent of the "machine age" of the Twentieth Century and the introduction of refrigeration did beer production reach its maximum. Of the four breweries operating in La Crosse at the outbreak of the Civil War, it is estimated that the total production was not more than 25,000 barrels per year. There are several reasons why production was not so great in those early years. First, the breweries operated only during the winter; lacking the means of refrigeration, they could only manufacture the beer in the cold weather, and store it in the bluff caves. Although the exact date is not known, it was sometime in the early 1860s that the La Crosse breweries first began using river ice for refrigeration. Storage houses were built by all the active brewers. Ice refrigeration was a great step forward. European brewers laughed at American tradesmen when they told their counterparts in the old country of the new method of storing beer. They said it couldn't be done, and they clung to the age-old method of letting nature provide the cooling facilities deep in the earth.

Another reason that production in that time period remained low was the lack of effective transportation. None of the local breweries had much of an outside market. That development—in great proportions—was yet to come.

Lack of machinery to do the most exacting tasks in the brewery was another reason for low production. All the work had to be done by hand; bottled beer was almost unheard of at that time. All beer was put up in wooden casks. Those breweries not having their own cooperage departments contracted local cooperage shops to make their casks for them, which in itself was another industry of that age.

Brewers of the Civil War era experienced a difficult time to survive the war period. The government placed a heavy tax of one dollar per barrel on all beer produced as an emergency measure, with a promise that it would not last much more than a year. But after three years it still remained. It was finally reduced to fifty cents per barrel by an act of congress.

With an investment of $25,000 at the close of the War, George Zeisler and Otto Nagel erected a three-story stone building along Third Street, and started the brewery that was later known as George Zeisler and Sons. First year production was 1,000 barrels. Two years later, Mr. Zeisler became sole owner of the business. His production increased in the next five years, demanding expansion and improvements to the plant. Then, in December, 1873 the structure caught fire and burned to the ground. Reconstruction began, and with plans of re-opening on July 4, 1874, the new plant caught on fire, but was only partially destroyed. The buildings were fully insured, so Zeisler suffered only the loss of time and consequent business. He rebuilt again, this time a four-story brick and stone structure at a cost of $35,000. Eight men were employed in the brewery at the time of re-opening, and 3,200 barrels of beer were produced each year. The John Gund Brewing Company bought the Zeisler brewery in 1902, a few months following George Zeisler's death.

John Gund dissolved his partnership with Gottlieb Heileman in the City Brewery in 1872, and the next year began construction of the Empire Brewing Company at Ninth Street and South Avenue, then only open prairie land. At the start, the Gund plant was only a small one, though much larger than his first brewery at Front and Division Streets. Over the years, it was practically rebuilt and received extensive additions to the extent that it might easily have been considered a completely new plant. His investment prior to 1890 was $250,000.

The enlarged brewery employed about 25 men in 1880. The use of ice for refrigeration made possible the expansion and it grew to such an extent that before 1880 the plant had two ice houses, one of which called for 1,300 tons of ice in the overhead ice room.

Ice houses of that time consisted of a basement, main floor, and an overhead ice room. Both basement and main floors were used for storage; they contained many great hogsheads of beer, each of which contained about 35-40 barrels, a barrel being 31 gallons. The ice buildings were well insulated and usually were connected with the brewing house, making convenient transportation of the new brew to the storage facility.

There is not much to be said about the growth of the G. Heileman Brewery in the early years following the Civil War. It is known that in 1860 when John Gund was still associated with the firm, 500 barrels of beer were produced per year. When he withdrew from the business, production had increased to 3,000 barrels annually.

Mr. Heileman died in 1878, but his wife continued to operate the business under the same company name for some time. The business continued to grow; 7,170 barrels of beer were produced in 1880; twelve men and three boys were employed. E.T. Mueller became the plant manager in 1884; he was Mr. Heileman's son-in-law.

The G. Heileman Brewing Company operated until nearly the end of the Twentieth Century.

The Eagle Brewery opened at Twelfth and La Crosse Streets the same year that Zeisler and Nagel started the brewery on North Third Street. This property changed hands several times in the next few years. It became known as the Franz Bartl Brewery in 1886. Production capacity increased at this brewery from 1,000 barrels in 1867 to about 10,000 in 1890.

The only known brewery to be operated in North La Crosse was the Voegele Brewery, later to be Erickson's or Monitor Brewery; its location was on Monitor Street at Copeland Avenue. John Erickson gained possession in 1898 and ran it until 1923.

5

APPLETON LIGHTS

Although it wasn't the first in the United States, Appleton, Wisconsin can be credited with the first electric generating plant in the West, providing electricity for the general public.

For quite some time, Thomas Edison had been developing the incandescent electric light and the equipment to supply the power. His system was tested in several private homes; then a central power station was put into service at Menlo Park, New Jersey in the winter of 1881-82 for demonstration purposes, but not until late 1882 was it available for public use.

The system had been tried in London, but was unsuccessful as a permanent installation. In the United States, however, the Edison Electric Illuminating Company of New York, organized in 1880, was busy laying the plans for a means of lighting the city with electricity, using the Edison central station system. Property on Pearl Street in New York was acquired and work began laying the underground conductors, but it would be September 4, 1882 when the Pearl Street station was put into operation.

During this same time period, the Western Edison Electric Light Company of Chicago was incorporated, and acquired territorial rights for Illinois, Wisconsin, and Iowa. Edison's electric lighting system was placed on the Western market in May 1882.

By July that year, the Chicago company had attracted the interest of a group of mill owners and other citizens of Appleton, Wisconsin; they were eager to experiment with the new lighting system, and they would soon make their city noteworthy in electricity history.

Led by H.J. Rogers, president of the Appleton Paper and Pulp Company, the group invited an engineer of the Western Edison Light Company to Appleton to explain the new system to the group of businessmen. They became quite intrigued by the possibilities of lighting their mills and their homes with electricity, and they were hopeful of making this "invisible power" available to the general public, as well.

Edison's engineer satisfied the Appleton investors; they contracted the Western Edison Light Company in mid-August to supply them with two water power driven Edison "K" dynamos with the capability to light 550 lamps. Sometime later, a construction man/ electrician was sent from Chicago to install the first generator at the paper company's mill. Installation took nearly six weeks; although it was not the first in the US, the Appleton system was the earliest use of a central station power plant in the West, and the first to be driven by water power. This mill and another mill a mile away, both owned by Appleton Paper and Pulp, as well as the newly constructed residence of Company President Rogers were wired.

There were rumors about this time that Mr. Rogers, who was also the president of the local gas company, had purchased the rights to the electric lighting system merely to keep it from competing with the gas business, and that he never intended to make it a public utility. On September 9, 1882, the *Appleton Crescent* newspaper disproved the rumors, reporting the wiring process at the mills and Rogers' home, and "if it proves an unquestioned success, as of course it cannot fail to, then the light will be substituted generally for gas in all our public and private buildings and the gas will be cheapened, used for heating, cooking, and running light machinery." Certainly, the businessmen who initiated the project were truly prophets and believers in American inventiveness.

Late September, the same newspaper announced that the mills would undergo a test of the new lighting system, and on Wednesday the 27th, all was ready, however, when the power was applied, the lights failed to glow. It was assumed that the failure was due to the high moisture caused by the steam from the mill. The Edison engineer was summoned from Chicago by telegraph; he quickly discovered some slight errors in the wiring arrangements, which were easily corrected. Saturday September 30, 1882, the dynamo was put into operation, and the hanging pear-shaped globes emitted the incredible, steady incandescent light. Observers declared the illuminated buildings to be "bright as day." The experiment was a great success; the confidence of the mill owners had been justified.

The test was then repeated at the Rogers residence with gratifying success; it was the first home in the West to be exclusively lighted by the Edison system.

As with the trial of any new mechanical system, problems did arise. The waterwheel used to drive the dynamo also drove some new machinery in the mill. Because of the varying load on the machines, so did the waterwheel and dynamo speed greatly vary. Sometimes the voltage rose so high that all the lamps in the circuit were burned out. After several of these incidents, the dynamo was moved to another location in the mill, and was driven by its own waterwheel.

The second dynamo of the contract was originally installed in the Vulcan mill at the opposite side of the city. The owners decided, however, to construct a building independent of the two mills at a point between them. The dynamos were then transferred to that location, and the quickly-erected frame shack became the first central station for commercial electricity production in the West, the predecessor of all the great generating plants that we know today. By December 1882, several more residences, the Appleton Blast Furnace, A.W. Patten's Paper Mill, Fleming's Linen Mill, and the Appleton Woolen Mill were all illuminated by Edison lights. The following January, lights were successfully installed in the Waverly Hotel, giving great satisfaction. The local newspaper boasted that Appleton then had more electrically lighted buildings than any other city in the United States.

Service was from dusk to daylight only; there were no meters to measure the usage of electricity, so patrons of the light utility paid a flat rate of $1.20 per month per lamp for all-night service. If used only until ten o'clock p.m., the rate was eighty-four cents per month. All customers purchased their own lamps at a cost of $1.60 each.

Because there was no fuse protection, the bare copper power lines were subject to short circuits, causing occasional power failure to the entire system. Wind, or anything out of the ordinary like a branch falling off a tree, if it fell against the wires, would create a short circuit, and the system would have to be shut down. All company hands then went out to find where the trouble was; sometimes it took an hour, sometimes a day, and in the meantime, there was no service.

By the 1920s, the Appleton Edison Light Company supplied electric service to fourteen surrounding municipalities and villages, and operated power lines over an area of more than fifty square miles.

Electric Railway

Not many people know that the electric railway had its start in Appleton, Wisconsin. F.E. Harriman, an Appleton real estate operator, instituted the first electric railway there in 1887. Constructed from east to west city limits traversing the main business area, it operated along that same route well into the Twentieth Century.

The proposed project was received with great skepticism, endless debate over its usefulness, and whether operating heavy cars with the invisible electric power could even be accomplished. The doubters were in large majority; failure was freely predicted. The promoter—Harriman—was looked upon as a dreamer and a visionary, but he maintained vigilant attention to the task until construction of the line was completed and the rolling stock arrived.

The announcement was made that power would be turned on and the cars would operate, the trial run commencing at the extreme east end of the line where there was a steep hill. A car was placed on the track, and the public was invited to witness the beginning of this new era.

Half of the population turned out to observe what they expected to be a failed venture; scoffers laughed at the presumption of anyone who believed sufficient power could be sent over a small copper wire to propel a heavy, loaded car up the hill.

A sufficient number of people from the assembled crowd were requested to board the car to take a free ride. The car was filled, and many even clung to the outside wherever footing could be secured. It was a crucial moment. Success or failure was imminent. Absolute silence prevailed. The crowd seemed to hold its breath.

The promoter, who envisioned great things from this, stood courageously beside the car. He raised his hand and gave the signal. Power was turned on by the motorman and the heavily loaded car jerked forward, slowly at first, and then gradually gained speed as it started off on the first journey ever made by an electrically propelled vehicle.

At that moment, a great industry was born that soon would become widespread across the country, and it would remain a pillar in transportation for many years to come. By 1922, in Wisconsin alone, more than 260,000,000 passengers had ridden the urban electric railways.

6

TAYCHEEDAH: VILLAGE BY THE LAKE

The first Europeans to explore the Lake Winnebago area found an Indian village on the southeast shore. The chief of this colony was Sar-ro-chau; he and his Winnebago band would be long remembered by all the early traders and settlers because of their friendly manner and their willingness to help the newcomers when other Indian tribes became hostile. The old chief took part in the War of 1812, and he died soon after. His son, Charatchou, aided the American militia in the pursuit of Black Hawk's warriors in 1832.

During the years of exploration and settlement of the Wisconsin Territory, the overland travel route from the Green Bay region to Fond du Lac and the prairies beyond followed the eastern shore of the expansive lake. Travelers passed through the old Indian camping grounds, and the pioneers became intrigued with the possibilities of this being the perfect location for a settlement. A mile of level land covered with groves of trees stretched back from the sandy shore of the lake to a picturesque, 200-feet-high ledge, with another extensive area of level, wooded land.

The view of the lake from this higher level was incredibly beautiful, and the entire area seemed ideal for a village or city.

A settlement was started at Taycheedah in 1839. The first permanent settler to build a home there was Francis D. McCarty, who was soon followed by more settlers from the east. He built and managed a hotel, later to be owned and operated by Nathaniel Perry until the old structure became inadequate to accommodate the many travelers who came to or passed through the village. Perry then built a much larger hotel, and under his management, this hostelry was known from Green Bay to Chicago for its genuine hospitality and the excellence of its meals.

B.F. and J.T. Moore opened the first general store in Taycheedah in 1841, serving the entire region northward to Brothertown. By 1850, a large flour mill and a sawmill operated in Taycheedah; the thriving village had also attracted a tin shop, dry goods stores, and two blacksmith shops.

Governor James Doty assisted in the construction of the first public schoolhouse of the county at Taycheedah in 1842, and the first school bell heard there was a gift from Col. Henry Conklin. He acquired the bell from the dismantled steamer *Advocate* that was wrecked on the Hudson River. Edgar Conklin was the teacher in this pioneer public school that served the population of both Taycheedah and Fond du Lac.

The beauty of the location seemed more attractive than

the earlier established Fond du Lac, and for a decade more than half of the prominent men of Fond du Lac County lived in Taycheedah. It became the social and cultural center of Fond du Lac County, and its commercial importance shadowed the neighboring settlement of Fond du Lac.

The shortcoming of Taycheedah was its harbor, never a good landing place for anything but smaller vessels. However, the first steamboat to navigate on Lake Winnebago waters, the *Manchester*, Capt. Stephen Hoteling, master, made its maiden voyage to Taycheedah, and the town became the southern terminal with Neenah the northern, and Oshkosh and Fond du Lac intermediate stopping ports.

Situated at the southernmost end of the lake, Fond du Lac's harbor was superior to that of Taycheedah, but there seemed little else to attract growth in the early times. The land was low and marshy, and to the early settlers there, the drainage problem must have been nearly insurmountable. Every spring when the snow melted from the surrounding hills, flooding occurred, creating a great disadvantage. However, the strategic location made Fond du Lac the more logical site for a city. In addition to the excellent harbor conditions, it was anticipated that the major railroad lines would likely converge there; that important factor apparently far outweighed the problems with the terrain.

Although Taycheedah was the larger community, the rivalry for supremacy continued through the 1840s. About 1848, however, Fond du Lac began to attract settlers in such numbers as to establish its domination for all time. This result was due largely to the prudence of Dr. Mason C. Darling. He had acquired enormous amounts of real estate at Fond du Lac, and donated a site for the courthouse as well as lots for many new businesses. At a time when money was scarce in this struggling new territory, businessmen were eager to take advantage of such offers of free land. Speculators in Taycheedah were still holding their building sites at premium prices, and therefore lost the edge.

The decline of Taycheedah started before the Civil War. Nearly all the old families that had been there in the beginning and had built Taycheedah to a thriving community were gone, moved to Fond du Lac and other cities, taking with them the businesses that had made the village prosper. But the village never completely vanished; as late as the 1920s, there was still a good public school, a Methodist Church, a general store, and a post office served a population of one hundred fifty people. Passengers could board trains that stopped on signal at a little weather-beaten shed, although there was no station agent or freight service. Today, homes and resorts garnish the lake shore for miles, and Taycheedah is as beautiful as it ever was.

7

DOOR COUNTY FORTRESS

Just up the coastline from Jacksonport in Door County, Hibbard Creek rambles through lowland on its way from the rocky inlands of the peninsula to gently wash over a sandbar into the big waters of Lake Michigan. It was there that the great village of the Potawatomi—Mechingan—once stood on the banks of Hibbard Creek. Mechingan was established following a ten-year war in which the Potawatomi subdued the Winnebago, forcing them to move southwestward to the shores of the big inland lake that now bears their name.

Then came a period of tranquility on the peninsula, however, it was not to last long. Another less-peace-loving eastern tribe, the Iroquois, would soon pose a serious threat, and tranquil Door Peninsula would become a battle ground.

The Potawatomi came from the northeast with the Ottawa and Ojibwa to the eastern shore of Lake Huron, probably around 1400 after the North American climate became colder. They eventually settled in the northern portion of lower Michigan. By then, the three tribes were separated, but there still remained the memory of their close alliance.

Their move to the west side of Lake Michigan occurred around 1630 when the Huron, Ottawa, and Tionantati had exhausted the beaver in their homelands and were forcefully seizing new hunting territory from the tribes in lower Michigan. It is unlikely that Jean Nicollet encountered the Potawatomi on his 1634 exploration of Wisconsin, as he followed the northern shore of Lake Michigan while enroute to Green Bay.

Because the Iroquois of New York were perhaps the most savage and vicious of all Indians, the French had carefully avoided selling arms and ammunition to them. But the Dutch did not practice such caution, as they were more interested in trade profits than preventing bloodshed. As soon as they had acquired the Dutch arms, they announced their intentions of exterminating their neighbors—red and white—for as far as they might travel in all directions. In just a few years they had destroyed countless Indian villages and had accumulated more than 50,000 scalps.

Tribes who were friendly to the whites, particularly the French, suffered the most. Without guns, they could not defend themselves against the Iroquois, and their only option was to flee westward. Some came to Green Bay, some stopped on Washington Island, and some followed a route around the south shore of Lake Michigan and did not rest until they reached central Wisconsin.

The Huron, who had stopped on Washington Island, just off the tip of the Door Peninsula, realized they were not completely safe there. Scouts had been sent back to spy on the Iroquois. When the first scouts returned in 1652, they brought only bad news: 800 Iroquois warriors were on their way with orders to track down the Huron and wipe them out. After that, they would destroy the French, and extend their predominance from the Atlantic to the Great Lakes.

Needless to say, panic was among the Huron people. They were unable to defend themselves, and evading the blood-thirsty Iroquois seemed futile. So with the Ottawa, they sent a delegation down to Mechingan in hopes that their Potawatomi friends would help them. In larger number, all of them together might be able to stand off the Iroquois, and perhaps, with the grace of the Great Spirit, be victorious over them.

The Potawatomi villagers showed passion for their allies and agreed to allow the refugees protection at Mechingan; within a few weeks, the population there rose from 1,500 to over 4,000.

Almost a year passed without any sign of the attackers. But the relentless Iroquois continued searching blindly through the strange country.

Mechingan was crowded, but with a triple stockade of stout timbers surrounding the village, it was secure. For months hunters had been bringing in deer, beaver, and fish. Maize and other vegetables had been harvested and carefully stored. The people were nervous, as the Iroquois were expected at any time, but they felt reasonably safe.

No one ventured very far beyond the village walls.

The Iroquois warriors did arrive, not expecting to find such a fortress that would not be easily penetrated. They were probably astonished at the sight, with thoughts that no village had ever held out long against them. But Mechingan and its inhabitants presented a new challenge. The Iroquois may have attempted an attack, but quickly learned that it was useless and a waste of ammunition. So they settled in to plan their siege.

As proficient as they were in battle, the Iroquois were alarmingly poor at hunting. Game in the surrounding forest was now scarce due to the skills of the Potawatomi, and the fish were nearly impossible to catch. The warriors had carried some corn with them on their long expedition, but it was gone.

Choosing humility over starvation, the invincible Iroquois agreed to release their prisoners and meekly asked for peace. The people of Mechingan graciously accepted the proposition, and promised that every member of the Iroquois war party would be given a corn cake upon leaving the country.

The generous offer to provide their enemies with all that precious food, however, was not exactly a simple gesture of forgiveness; the Huron and Ottawa had been chased by the Iroquois far too long to only call the whole thing even. They poisoned every cake, and every Iroquois warrior might have died in agony. But when the cakes were tossed over the stockade walls, the chief ordered them to be left untouched. He picked up one and fed it to a hungry dog. Within a few minutes, the dog fell dead.

If the mighty Iroquois were humiliated when they were forced by hunger to seek a peaceful conclusion, now they lost all dignity. Silently they packed up and left. Some went north, only to fall into a trap set by the Ojibwa and were nearly destroyed. The others went south into Illinois country where the Illinois met them with such force as to nearly wipe them out. Only a few stragglers eventually made it back to New York. The Iroquois rampage was over, and peace on the Door Peninsula resumed.

8

PAUL SEIFERT—FOLK ARTIST

For several decades around the turn of the twentieth century, a German immigrant named Paul Seifert traveled through rural Southwest Wisconsin, stopping at different homesteads and chatting with the owners. He complimented each farmer on his property and before long convinced him that his place was picture-perfect and should be immortalized in a painting. Seifert, of course, would be just the man for the job. For about three dollars, he promised a beautiful watercolor on 21" x 28" paper. Seifert's sales pitch must have been convincing, and his paintings became so popular that eventually over a hundred of his rural scenes were displayed in farm houses all over Richland, Sauk, Grant, Iowa, and Crawford counties. In one case, Seifert even painted six versions of the same farm. Today Paul Seifert's paintings are highly appreciated as examples of rural Midwestern folk art.

Paul Seifert arrived in Wisconsin in 1867, and for the rest of his life he remained closely connected with the land and the people of the state's Driftless Region. Born in 1846 in Dresden, Saxony, he grew up surrounded by teachers and students at the Free Mason Institute in Dresden, a preparatory boarding school for boys where his father was the head schoolmaster. Paul Seifert later attended a trade school (the exact school and trade are unknown), and—just prior to his emigration—also the Royal Academy for Agriculture and Forestry in Tharand, Saxony, for one semester. A photo labeled "winter semester 1866/67" shows Paul Seifert in his student uniform at the Academy.

These were turbulent times in Europe and especially in the Kingdom of Saxony. In 1866, decisive battles in the Austro-Prussian War were fought on Saxon territory, with Saxon troops fighting on the losing Austrian side. In 1867, as a result, Saxony lost some of its previous independence and became a member of the newly founded North German Federation, the precursor of the German Empire, which was dominated by Prussia.

It is not known if the political and military situation influenced Paul Seifert to emigrate, but on September 14, 1867 he boarded the ship *Eugenie* in Hamburg and two days later sailed for America. The *Eugenie* arrived in New York on November 2, and Paul quickly moved on to Richland City in Richland County, Wisconsin. In 1867, Richland City was a boomtown at the confluence of the Wisconsin River and the Pine River, a major stopping point for riverboats between Prairie Du Chien and Portage. Today the city no longer exists, having been abandoned because of a river that continually changed its course.

Paul Seifert quickly adapted to his new surroundings. He befriended a German family, the Krafts, who had come to Richland City from Baden via New York, and in 1868,

Seifert married their daughter, Elizabeth. Together the young couple bought land nearby, started a vegetable garden, and sold their produce in neighboring communities. A year later, the first of their four daughters was born.

With many mouths to feed, Seifert made a living for himself and his family in various ways. He opened a taxidermy studio, and—while Elizabeth and his daughters tended the vegetable farm—traveled the Wisconsin countryside with a sketch pad, paper, pencils, and paint. Sometimes he created a painting on the spot, while at other times he made a sketch and finished the work at home. His most productive decade was the 1880s. His earliest known farmscape was painted in 1879; his last may have been painted in the late 1910s, as it includes a 1915 Ford Model T. Seifert depicted rural life as a simple but detailed tableau. That could include colorful barns and houses; farmers' children playing in the field; someone shooting a fox nearby; lazy cows grazing in the meadow behind a barn—a beautiful and idyllic world, without the hardship that farming in the late-nineteenth century also entailed.

In the late 1940s, Paul Seifert's watercolors were discovered by Jean Lipman, a prominent folk-art scholar and long-time editor of *Art in America* magazine. She not only wrote about them in her many publication, but also started collecting Seifert paintings herself. Before long the watercolor farmscapes from Wisconsin became sought-after collectors' items across the nation.

While Paul Seifert is remembered today mostly for his

paintings of farms, he was also keenly interested in the history, the landscape, and the people of Southwest Wisconsin. In particular, he was fascinated by Native Americans. On his many excursions throughout the region, he found and collected Native American artifacts. Many of these, such as projectiles and scrapers, he donated to the Wisconsin Historical Society and regional museums.

Maybe that is why his name is connected with one of the "cave mysteries" in the region. After Seifert's death in 1921, stories appeared in Wisconsin papers, citing an article that purportedly had been printed years earlier in Vienna, Austria. As the tale goes, Paul Seifert had stumbled upon a hidden cave in the Wisconsin River bluffs filled with skeletons and Native American artifacts. He had sent some of the objects to an archeologist friend in Vienna, who supposedly travelled all the way to Wisconsin, inspected the cave for himself, and was stunned by the treasure he saw. After that visit, however, Seifert destroyed the entrance to the cave to hide it and its contents forever. His friend returned to Europe, and Seifert never shared the location with anybody else. This story was often told in connection with other stories of Indians who had "vanished" in the bluffs. Fact or fiction, people are still looking to find the "Indian mystery cave" in the bluffs of Richland County.

9

BOGUS BILLS

Wisconsin, to almost everyone, is known as the home of many things such as cheese, first Super Bowl Champions, birthplace of the Republican Party, and the invention of the typewriter. But it may come as surprise to some that Wisconsin was the Nineteenth Century counterfeiting capital of North America. Two major gangs of counterfeiters—or "koniackers" as they were called then—operated in Southwestern Wisconsin, and were the shrewdest operators that the U.S. Secret Service had ever encountered.

The following narrative is a three-part newspaper series authored by Captain Patrick D. Tyrell of the U.S. Secret Service, his first-hand experience, as it appeared in syndication in 1905. (Note: the newspaper in which this article was published is old and difficult to read; some words and characters are faded or obliterated. Attempts have been made to duplicate Tyrell's story as closely as possible.)

The Boscobel Koniackers
Part 1

It was one day in the early spring of the year 1878 that a young man signing the application form as "George C. King

No. 873 West Adams street, Chicago Ill" appeared at the money order windows at the Chicago post office and asked for two money orders aggregating $75 in amount, payable to A.J. Williams of Canandaigua, N.Y. With the application he handed the clerk a $100 note. The clerk made out the money orders, gave them and $25 to the applicant and the latter disappeared. The same day in counting the cash received at the money order window the chief encountered the $100 note and became suspicious of its genuineness. It purported to be a note of the issue of the Revere National Bank of Boston.

Being notified that such a note had been received at the post office, I immediately made an examination of it and pronounced it counterfeit. I then took possession of the note and submitted it to Fred M. Blount, who was then the cashier in the United States sub-(*****) in Chicago for him to place the government "counterfeit" stamp on it. This he refused to do on the grounds that the note, in his opinion, was genuine. I pointed out many discrepancies between the note in hand and one known to be genuine, but Blount claimed he frequently noticed discrepancies as great between two genuine notes of the same issue.

On his refusal to stamp the note I took it to Thomas P. Tallman, cashier of the Trader's national bank, whom I considered the most reliable expert in such matters in any of the city banks. Mr. Tallman spent two hours making a minute examination of the note, and at the end of that time concurred with my original opinion that the note was counterfeit. Having been thoroughly satisfied in my own mind from the beginning the note was spurious, I deemed it important to trace it. From the post office records the name and address given by the passer of the note were secured, and these were found to be correct.

King was not at home when I called at his house, but from his wife I learned he had received a $100 bill from A.J. Williams, a friend of her husband's in Canandaigua, N.Y. The passing of the note had been noted in my daily report to chief Brooks in Washington, and as soon as I learned the note had been received from the same man to whom the money orders purchased with it, I suggested that the eastern division of the secret service take up the New York end of the chain.

The following day I arrested King at the La Salle Street offices in which he was employed and found in his possession a letter from his Canandaigua friend. The letter itself was an innocent, friendly missive, but in the envelope was a separate note instructing King to buy the money orders, keep $25 for himself and to "keep his own counsel". In my mind there was no reasonable doubt that Williams, who was a jeweler, and King at least had guilty knowledge that the note in question was counterfeit.

* * * *

In glancing back over a long line of records for the years 1878 and 1879, I select the foregoing incident as the first thread the secret service picked up in the skein of events which afterward connected east and west in a gigantic "koniacking" swindle that reached into the United States Treasury building itself; and I set it forth here merely on account of its intrinsic importance.

At the present day, when the counterfeiting of the nation's money is rapidly passing into the category of lost arts, the younger generation will wonder at the extent of counterfeiting a third of a century ago as indicated by the narratives I have told and the one I am about to relate. And if there be any wonder on this score there will be greater when I say that Nelson Driggs, Ben Boyd, Fred Blebuah, "Pete" McCartney and a score of others already mentioned were members of the western contingent only, while in the east was a corresponding number just as skilled and just as active.

The connections between east and west crossed and interlaced until they formed a figurative free-masonry of counterfeiting reaching from ocean to ocean and from Canada to the gulf. For this condition there was a most obvious explanation. We whose hairs are grey will remember when the necessities of government during the war of the rebellion compelled the issue of hundreds of millions in legal tender of new and various kinds. These issues were made hastily, being demanded by the exigencies of the kaleidoscopic financial situation, and were imperfect to an extent that would now be considered ridiculous.

Much of the new currency issued during the war and the existence of the state banks was not only defective in the engraving, but was printed on paper which could be easily duplicated by a clever chemist. Scrip was in use, and the government product, from the engraver's standpoint, was not of a high character. In short the large spawn of "koniackers" that did so much unlawfully to inflate the currency from 1850 to 1880 were bred by temptation arising from the defective national currency – defective from the artisan's point of view.

The eastern and western crowds operated largely each for itself without the help of the other, but the resources of the east were drawn on when the western counterfeiters needed a new plate or material not obtainable in their own bailiwick, and the easterners frequently came west for similar accommodations. "Coney" floated in the cast was frequently traced to the Mississippi valley or farther west, and in some of the most troublesome imitations we ever had to deal with in the west were the handiwork of eastern artisans. With this explanation I will take up another thread in the story of **"The Boscobel Koniackers."**

* * * *

Sometime before my story opens A. L. Drummond chief secret service operative in charge of New York division, had run across plates for the manufacture of scrip which he had traced to the hand of Kale Ellis, a western product, and as desperate a counterfeiter as ever dodged the secret service. Drummond and W.W. Kennoch, another operative, both had been sailors, and, through furnishing information to the revenue officers concerning certain smuggling operations, had been appointed customs officers in New York. From this work they went into the Secret Service

Woods was then the chief of the service and had sent Drummond to Wisconsin to hunt down Ellis, the maker of the scrip plate. Drummond caught up with his man and Ellis fled with the Secret Service officer in close pursuit. The counterfeiter ran to the Pecatonica River, plunged in, and swam to the other bank. Drummond, seeing his man escaping, fired at him in midstream, one of the bullets clipping away the lobe of Ellis' right ear making a mark of identification became known to every man in the Secret Service.

In his flight Ellis has carried with him the plates from which the script was being made, and, knowing he could not be convicted unless the plates were found in his possession he dropped the package in the river as he swam for his life. With remarkable presence of mind, while bullets from the officer's revolver were clipping the water all around him, Ellis mentally took such accurate bearings of the spot at which he dropped the package that he was able afterwards to recover it.

He reached the opposite bank exhausted. Drummond followed him over and searched him, but found him "clean" – that is, without tangible evidence of his guilt in his possession. Aware he could not make a case that would hold up in court against Ellis, Drummond let him go, but not until the counterfeiter had delivered this message for the benefit of all of us: "If any **** Secret Service man ever again tries to take me I will kill him on sight."

* * * *

Ellis was known throughout the service as a man of great determination and disregard of consequences when it came to keeping his skin whole, and his sworn threat to Drummond made him a man to be feared unless we took him unawares. I was comparatively young in the service and very ambitious. I decided that Ellis was in my territory, and as he was a particularly dangerous customer, besides having escaped from one of the best operatives in the department, it would be much to my credit if I captured him, and at the same time would rid the public of a sagacious counterfeiter.

By systematic "piping" and the use of "stool pigeons" I learned in the early part of 1875 that Ellis was one of a band of "coney" men who were running off a big issue of scrip in the town of Boscobel, in central western part of Wisconsin.

Despite the studied and artful secrecy of the counterfeiters it is true that seldom was a big issue of "coney" that floated without the secret service having some knowledge of the forthcoming event. The "shoving" of an issue was always preceded by the absolute retirement of the manufacturers and the mysterious activity on the part of the dealers. In other words, the coming event got into the wind, and, we may have no definite knowledge whatsoever, we could scent the approaching in cases by keeping in touch with the different men who were always under suspicion. In this case it was learnt that Napoleon B. Latta, a wealthy French farmer living 15 miles from Boscobel, had contracted with the Ellis crowd for all the "coney" of a certain standard of excellence. We even got so far into the secrets of the "coney" men as to learn that Latta was to pay 35 cents in genuine money for each dollar of representative currency, which by the way, was an unusually high price, as the market quotation in those days for a good quality of "coney" was 17 cents on the dollar.

In the spring of 1878, therefore, I went to Boscobel. Registering at the hotel under a false name and from a small town in Missouri, I kept pretty much to myself and out of sight. In order to keep the landlord from becoming inquisitive, as the landlords of hotels in small towns are prone to do, I asked him a number of questions concerning the opportunity for successfully loaning money on farms in the vicinity. These questions had the desired effect of preventing others from asking me questions which I might arouse suspicion by not answering.

* * * *

In the engraving department of the United States Government there is an elaborate system of screens, reflectors and shades by which is obtained the peculiar soft light necessary to the engraving of plates from which currency is printed. By counterfeiters this system must be imitated as closely as limited facilities permit, and I believe to this day I could pick out any house in which counterfeiting was being carried on in any town of such size as would allow the inspection of all the houses.

Boscobel was not so large but that it was easy to locate the rendezvous of the counterfeiters. As usual it was on the outskirts of town and its nearest neighbor was 100 yards away. There was but one house beyond it on the street. The house was a two-story frame structure. The peculiar arrangement of the curtains on the second floor told the tale without any other information.

Malcolm Robinson and his wife occupied the house by themselves, according to the beliefs of the townspeople. The facts were, however, as revealed by investigation, that Robinson and his wife occupied the lower story and Kale Ellis and Franklin J. Brown the upper story. The three men were counterfeiters. Robinson was the manufacturer of the Boscobel crowd, Brown being the printer under Robinson's direction. Ellis was the engraver, as I have previous told, but at that particular time he was also aiding in the work of running off the issue for the use of "Nap" Latta.

Brown and Ellis seldom went downstairs, and were never seen by the neighbors, their meals being served them upstairs by Mrs. Robinson. The little exercise they got was taken at night. The life of the counterfeiter at his busy times is not a bed of roses, by any means, for it requires the utmost concentration and application of effort. The longer the delay in producing an issue the greater danger of discovery, and such a task, once begun, is followed with tremendous diligence until the output is in the hands of the dealer and the genuine coin of the realm safely in the hands of the manufacturers of the "coney."

* * * *

I took some time to satisfy myself as to the exact conditions in and around the Robinson residence. I had not forgotten Kale Ellis' little pleasantry in regard to the probable fate of any secret service men who attempted to capture him, and I did not intend to take any more chances than necessary when it came to planning for the event. But the time soon came when it seemed certain no mistake could be made in raiding the Robinson house.

Part 2

Frank W. Oakley, United States Marshal at Madison, was told of my plan and his services and those of two of his most competent deputies were secured. Warrants were taken out secretly at Madison. Marshal Oakley said he had frequently heard of Kale Ellis, and that from all he had heard he was a dangerous man to handle. I also sent to Chicago for John McDonald and C.D. Townsend, the latter being a secret service operative. The five men were instructed to come to Boscobel on the same day and to register at the hotel without letting it be known that they knew me or knew one another.

It was about 11 o'clock at night when I smuggled them into my room, where I outlined my plan to them. I did not deem it consistent to send any other man into probable danger of which I myself was afraid, so I planned to take the lead in the actual entry of the house. One of the others was to be stationed 16 feet from each corner of the house in such a way that each could command a view of two sides of the building. I calculated that Ellis and Brown might leap from the second-story windows in front when they heard me ascending the stairs. To the men stationed in front I said: "One of these men who may jump from the second-story has sworn to kill on sight any secret service man that tries to take him. His record is such there is no doubt he means what he says. If these men jump from the windows they will be armed and will kill any men in their path. Either you or they will be killed. It will be better if it be they. Shoot them before they strike the ground if you want to save you lives."

* * * *

The nearest neighbors of the Robinson's had a child that was not expected to make it through the night on which we planned the raid. Mrs. Robinson, although the wife of one criminal and the associate of the others, retained the maternal solicitude for any child that was sick and had made herself useful at the house of her neighbors. She had been at the bedside of the little one during the day and had returned only in time to prepare supper for her husband and the other "koniackers". I knew of her interest in the condition of the sick child, and decided to turn it to our own advantage. At a quarter to two in the morning of April 16, 1875, we left the hotel and repaired to the Robinson home in such a manner as not to attract attention from any belated townsmen in case we met one.

After reaching the premises no word was spoken and none was necessary, as final and detailed instructions had been received by the officers before we left the hotel covering any possible emergency that might arise. The night was very dark and a high wind blew, suiting our purpose well.

With each man at his station, I rapped at the front door softly, one of the deputy marshals who was recommended for his coolness and bravery at my back. There was no answer and I knocked again, lightly, as I wished to avoid waking the men sleeping upstairs. Still there was no response, and the third time I rapped harder. Robinson came to the door. Without opening it he asked "Who's there?" "The child is worse" I answered. At this he opened the door carefully, but wide enough to enable me to get my foot through the opening and force a quick entrance. The deputy at my back was as dependable as I had been told he was, for he followed instructions to the letter, pressing in behind me and taking Robinson off my hands so that I could be free to go after the others. In a flash he had Robinson under cover of his revolver, and threatened him with death if he made any outcry.

The taking of Robinson had occurred in the little front hallway from which the stairs led to the second floor. Revolver in one hand and dark lantern in the other, I ran softly up the stairs. The door of the room in which the other two counterfeiters slept was ajar. Throwing the glare of the bull's-eye into the room I saw Ellis and Brown in bed, but both reaching for his revolver, one of the weapons being under the pillow and the other on a small stand at the head of the bed. Covering them with my own weapon before they had time to lay hands on their revolvers, I shouted: "lie back or I will kill you". Both lay on the pillows. "The first one that moves will be shot" I commanded.

Cautiously and with my revolver and lantern still trained on the counterfeiters I backed to the front window and rapped on the pane. This was the signal that had been arranged for two men to come to my assistance. Under the cover of three revolvers Ellis and Brown were doggedly obedient and put on their clothes. The other two men had by this time entered the house and gone in relief of the deputy who entered with me in caring for Robinson and his wife.

In the room across the hall from the sleeping room of Ellis and Brown I found the printing press and materials they had been using, $15,000 in 50 cent scrip, together with the same plates Kale Ellis had dropped in the Pecatonica river, in making his daring escape from Operative Drummond long before.

The three cursing counterfeiters, Mrs. Robinson and the "koniacking" outfit were taken to Madison on the next train. The men pleaded guilty and were sentenced to serve seven years in the penitentiary. Mrs. Robinson was given her liberty.

* * * *

Well satisfied with the results of the Wisconsin job, I returned to Chicago and dropped into the routine of my work, little thinking that the events immediately to follow would necessitate my return to the Badger State. But no sooner had I returned than a $100 note was brought to my attention which had been sent to the Union National bank from the City bank of Portage Wisconsin, a correspondent of the Chicago bank. The bill, in my opinion, was unquestionably counterfeit. A few days later a $100 bill of the same issue, but bearing the name of another bank, was offered at the Chicago Post office. Then to the Trader's National Bank came a $100 bill from the bank at Shelbyville, Illinois. This was also of the same issue, but bore the name of still another bank. My collection was soon further increased by a $100 bill from Parsons, Kansas, following which came the information from the secret service that a $100 note had been passed at Louisiana, Mo.

Here was an unexpected shower. The bills were apparently all off the same plate, which had been a skeleton plate, the names of the Revere national bank of Boston, Second national of Wilkes-Barre, PA., and the Merchant's national of New Bedford, Mass., having been filled in by the skeleton process. At the United States sub-treasury Fred M. Blount, the cashier, insisted the bills were genuine. The cashiers of five out of eight banks to which they were submitted also held them to be good. Thomas P. Tallman, cashier of the Traders' national, and I insisted they were counterfeit.

I found at the post office that the bill offered there had been sent by the postmaster at Cambridge Ill., to whom I immediately sent a telegram in the name of J.W. Palmer, the Chicago postmaster. The Cambridge postmaster answered that he had received the bill in question from the Cambridge bank and that no accurate description of the man who had passed it could be obtained. The cashier at the bank at Portage wrote that he had received the bill from a man about 45 years old, nearly six feet tall and with dark, full beard. He looked like a well to do farmer, the cashier wrote, but further than this the description was hazy. A somewhat similar general description, except as to the color of the beard and altogether more definite came from Parsons. I sent Operative Kennoch to St. Louis and Louisiana to pursue the investigation there.

* * * *

While these things were happening I received word through the United States Marshal at Springfield, Ill., to the effect that a deputy sheriff at Vandalia, Ill., had arrested a man trying to pass a $100 counterfeit bill at the Farmers' and Merchants' national bank in the latter city. This bit of news, considering in connection with the rapidly occurring events of the days previous, was decidedly important, and I lost no time in getting to Vandalia. I found at all bearded, farmer looking man of about 50 had tendered a $100 bill to David Palmer of the local bank and that Palmer had declined to accept it, reporting the matter to Deputy Sheriff Cluxton, who arrested the stranger at the railroad station as he was about to leave Vandalia. He gave the name "Levi Logan" and said he received the bill from one Charles Scott, of Fond du Lac, Wis., in a horse trade. When arrested he had in his possession another counterfeit bill of the same kind as he tried to pass, and $154 in good money.

I questioned the prisoner but decided from his manner that he was not "Levi Logan". Who he really was remained to be found out. I asked permission to take the prisoner into my custody but Deputy Sheriff Cluxton declined to turn him over to me. I argued that if held and tried in that county he could not possibly be convicted because witnesses could not be brought in from another state, whereas, the government could command the attendance of witnesses from any state. The local authorities also had no facilities for doing the work necessary to secure such evidence as would convict the prisoner. But Cluxton was obdurate. I appealed to a prominent local attorney who had influence with the deputy sheriff, and in this way finally secured custody of the prisoner and took him to Springfield.

I often have thought since that if the deputy who clung so tenaciously to his man had any idea the part the prisoner was to play in counterfeiting history he would have relinquished him gladly to the United States authorities. Had he persisted in retaining custody of "Levi Logan" it is likely that one of the most important bands of "koniackers" in the country would have enjoyed their liberty much longer than they did.

The only clues I had to work on in establishing the identity of "Levi Logan" were his story that he had come from Wisconsin, and a description of the man. The first clue was strengthened by the fact that the bills that had found their way into Chicago had been passed by a man traveling from north to south. I was convinced that "Logan" was an adept in the "shoving" of counterfeits, and if this were true and he hailed from Wisconsin there was little probability that he was not affiliated with the Boscobel gang in that state.

In the meantime the bill on the Revere National Bank of Boston had been received at the Chicago post office from George C. King, as told at the beginning of this story. This bill had come from the east, and from this fact I surmised that the man who passed it had traveled west to Wisconsin, probably from New York City, and thence southward.

I believed that in a region that had harbored for years such a strong band of counterfeiters as the Boscobel crowd there must be information concerning the identity of a "shover" who said he came from that locality, and who, apparently, was thoroughly familiar with it. Consequently I provided myself with photographs of "Levi Logan" and started for Wisconsin.

* * * *

On this trip I had not long pursued my investigation when I encountered the name "Watson" – one with which I was entirely unfamiliar in counterfeiting circles. From the report I got from persons familiar with Kale Ellis, Frank

Brown, and Malcolm Robinson, the "Watsons" must have visited Wisconsin frequently, always associating with men who bore shady reputations, and who later were found to be counterfeiters. The reputed home of the "Watsons" was at Clear Lake, IA. Without going to that place I stored away what I had heard about them for future reference, continuing my search in Wisconsin.

At last I found my reward through casually showing the photograph of "Levi Logan" to a man who at once recognized him as the father of Mrs. Malcolm Robinson. The true name of the Springfield prisoner I found to be Frank Conway. One of his daughters had married Malcolm Robinson and another had married is brother, Clate, both of the husbands being in prison for counterfeiting offenses.

Part 3

The further identification of Conway was simple matter. I found he had affiliated with counterfeiters for many years, and in 1876 had been arrested for horse stealing and convicted, carrying his case to the Supreme Court. After securing his freedom on bail he had disappeared from his Wisconsin haunts. He had been an associate of the mysterious "Watson brothers", and had visited them at their farm at Clear Lake. Further than this he had been closely connected with the band of "koniackers" that made headquarters in St. Paul. In short, the connection between the "Watsons", Conway, the Boston gang and the St. Paul counterfeiters was found to be very close, although the theft of the team of horses in Watseka County, Minnesota, was the only fact discovered that could be used against Conway at the forthcoming trial.

The defense of Conway at the trail was that "Charles Scott" whom he subpoenaed, had given him the bill, Scott testified to this fact. Conway admitted he had been arrested, and said after his arrest he had come to Chicago and then gone to New York, assuming the name L.C. Lavaree. He remained in New York a year, he said, and then returned to Wisconsin.

His defense availed him nothing and he was sentenced to five years. In the meantime the case in Parsons, Kan., had been made and he served another five years for that offense. Subsequently he was given another five years for horse stealing.

* * * *

With Conway "settled" in the penitentiary an investigation was made to determine the identity of the "Watsons". While it had not been proved, there was little doubt that Conway had gone east for the purpose of establishing a connection with one of the bands of counterfeiters which infested the Atlantic seaboard, that he had undertaken to "shove" some of the "coney" that was being issued by them. To a secret service man it was also clear that such a man as Conway, who had never been east before his arrest for horse stealing, could not have formed such a connection without taking with him first-class references from counterfeiters in the west who were well acquainted with the more prominent men in that line in the east.

From all I could gather of Conway's record he had not been associated before his eastern trip with men in the west who were on close terms with the eastern counterfeiting aristocrats. The high artistic character of the $100 bills he had "shoved" in the Mississippi valley was indication sufficient that they had come from the hands of artisans of much skill. In establishing the identity of the "Watson" brothers therefore, we hoped to be able to determine who had placed Conway in touch with the eastern counterfeiters and eventually uncover the makers of the $100 plate.

To relate the details of this investigation would consume more time and space than I have at my disposal, and I shall, therefore state that the "Waltons" were found to have been the Ballard brothers – Thomas, George, and John. In the annals of counterfeiting in the United States the name of Thomas Ballard must stand out most prominent, and I shall take the liberty of telling enough about this remarkable criminal character to give my readers some conception of his importance in "koniacking" history.

First, let not the members of the Masonic fraternity be shocked when I say that Thomas Ballard, at the summit of his success as a counterfeiter, was the master of Park Lodge, A.F.& A.M., in New York City. He came of good family, never smoked a cigar nor took a drink of intoxicating liquor, was married to an estimable woman, and, like many of his kind, was a model family man. He was born in New York State in 1819, and learned the trade of fancy carriage painting. When 18 years old he went to work for Henry Hinman, a wealthy carriage builder of New York City, and related by marriage to Joshua D. Miner, a prominent New York politician and city contractor. Hinman observed the genius of young Ballard and induced him to learn the trade of banknote making, at which he served four years.

Aided by Miner, Ballard obtained valuable information from the engraving department of the government. In 1862 produced for Miner and Henry C. Cole a plate of the one dollar United States treasury. His next was a plate of the two-dollar bills of the National Shoe & Leather bank of New York. From that he went to $10 counterfeits of three National banks of Poughkeepsie, the $20 bill of the Shoe & Leather bank, and then to the $100 and $500 "old issue" United States treasury notes.

Ballard had a comfortable residence at No. 235 West Fifty-Third Street, and here was supposed to be a painter. He left home every morning at seven o'clock to go to the carriage factory, in which he was interested, but instead of going there he went to No. 256 Riverton Street, where his brother John lived, and where the counterfeiting plant was located. The neighbors at No. 256 Riverton street believed Ballard to be a watchman in the custom house, and he left there regularly in the evening to go "to work", but in reality went home. He lived this dual life without detection for years.

The government at the time had a contract with the Glenn mills at West Chester, Pa., for its entire output of the celebrated "fiber" paper, the mills being run under supervision of government officials to prevent the paper or the secret of its manufacture being stolen. Ballard, in addition to being a high class engraver, was the only man in the world who could successfully make this paper outside the Glenn mills. As an engraver, chemist, papermaker and ink manufacturer Ballard was unexcelled. The treasury officials and money experts generally believed the "fiber" paper to be a complete guard against counterfeiting, and they were amazed at the product of Thomas Ballard long before such a man was known to the secret service. The presses of Hinman, Miner, and Ballard turned out bogus money in such amounts that the lawful currency became disparaged, and the capture of the makers of the clever counterfeits became a matter of imperative importance. He was caught in 1871, broke jail soon afterward, and his subsequent history would fill a good sized volume.

Arrested in Buffalo for engraving a plate of a $500 treasury note, which was pronounced superior to the genuine, Ballard was sent to Auburn penitentiary from which institution he escaped. While in Buffalo he had also worked on a plate with which he said he was going "to bankrupt Canada," and from the perfection of the work he seemed in fair way to make good on his intention.

In 1875 he was sentenced to serve 30 years in the penitentiary, after having been at large about three years with a standing reward of $5,000 for his capture. In 1878 he ripped open his own abdomen and severed an intestine in trying to take his own life, but recovered. A year later he drew a sharp knife across his throat severing the windpipe and muscles of the neck, and again recovered.

It was during the wanderings following Thomas Ballard's first arrest and while the reward of $5,000 was hanging over him that he and his two brothers came west and took up their residence on a farm near Clear Lake, Iowa. They assumed the family name Watson, and, naturally, fell into association with the counterfeiters operating in the northwest. They became acquainted with the Boscobel and St. Paul gangs, and with Frank Conway, which fact accounts for the frequency with which I encountered the assumed family name of the Ballards while trying to identify the man who had been arrested in Vandalin. The St. Paul contingent of counterfeiters had in their possession, it was afterward found, the Poughkeepsie and Peakskill plates that had been made in the east by Ballard and had issued money from them. There was no evidence that the Ballards accomplished much in the line of producing "coney" while in the west.

Before closing this narrative I wish to say that when the Ballards left Clear Lake Ia. to return to the east they buried ten sets of plates near the farm house they had occupied. This burial was according to the ironclad rule of "good" counterfeiters never to carry such evidence with them. Other counterfeiters however knew where they were hid, and five sets found their way into the possession of George Woolsey and Samuel Pizer, of the particular "koniacking" outfit known as the St. Paul crowd, and in August 1875 I had the satisfaction of arresting these shifty gentlemen and of confiscating these plates, $8,000 in representative currency and counterfeiting press, inks and papers. I do not know what became of the other five sets of plates after the Ballards buried them.

The end

The other band of "koniackers" made their headquarters in Monroe, Wisconsin, led by Napoleon Bonaparte Latta. The following article describing their capture appeared in the *Chicago Tribune*, July 12, 1871.

Capture of Five Noted Coneymen at Monroe, Wisconsin Seizure of $10,000 in Counterfeit National Bank Notes

Within the last two or three months the detectives of the United States Secret Service have captured quite a number of counterfeiters, and effectually stopped them from circulating bogus National' Bank and Treasury notes. The arrest of the Cleveland gang, a short time since was of great importance but it becomes insignificant when compared with the disbandment of a clan in Wisconsin which was accomplished last Friday by Chief Operative Lonergan and Detective Anderson of this city. About the 1st of January last, information was received by Lonergan that the "Bonelatta gang" were doing an extensive business in Wisconsin, and, as complaints came in almost weekly, a plan of operations for the capture of the counterfeiters was agreed upon. This gang numbered about forty men, who operated in Missouri, Kansas, Illinois, Wisconsin, Michigan, Minnesota, Texas, and New Mexico.

The chief of the gang a Napoleon Bonaparte Latta, better known as "Bonelatta " is a very astute individual, having served on the detective force of this city when Bradley was Superintendent. Nearly every detective in the employ of the Secret Service Department, noted for his skill in ferreting out "coney" men, had been put on his track, but, being acquainted with all the subterfuges and ruses adopted by officers to capture criminals, Latta was continually on his guard, and readily became aware of what was going on around him. By this knowledge he has escaped arrest for fifteen years, having carried on the business of a dealer in counterfeit money for that time.

The headquarters of the gang was at Monroe, the county seat of Green County, Wisconsin. Latta, who is quite wealthy, was, as he gave out, engaged in the hop-pole business. He and his associates never appeared to do anything, and it was a mystery to the citizens of the place how they got money, of which they always had plenty. Latta frequently left town, and it was soon ascertained by the detectives on his track that he visited St. Louis, or one of the other cities, and met rough looking men, who left the place as soon as Latta did. On these trips Latta would sell large sum of counterfeit money, principally to Texas men, who gave him gold in return for the bogus bills, at the rate of from 20 to 28 cents on the dollar.

In order to effect his arrest and that of his associates, and to collect evidence which would make their conviction certain, great caution was necessary. The detectives who had been sent to Monroe before were not cautious, and their presence in the place was reported to Latta immediately upon their arrival, and he was thereby enabled to avoid any of the traps set to catch him. He had men posted at the railroad depot and at the stage office, whose business it was to "shadow" every stranger and learn what brought him to Monroe and all about his antecedents. As these men were familiar with most of the government detectives, they were as quiet as mice when one came. Those they did not know, "gave themselves away" by their actions, and were obliged to leave without doing anything. About three weeks ago Anderson, ordinarily dressed, with a peddler's pack full of a patent soap, made his appearance in the town, and forthwith took possession of a street corner and commenced to dispose of the article to the people. He saw a man follow him from the railroad depot, and conducted himself in such a manner as to arouse no suspicion. Latta came along and looked at him sharply, but Anderson talked so well about the excellence of his soap as to completely disguise his true character. He sold the soap on the street for a week, a box of it coming to his hotel every other day. Keeping his eyes upon Latta, he soon discovered that the headquarters of the gang were in the saloon. Obtaining possession of a room in the adjoining building; he was able to overhear the plans of the .counterfeiters, and obtained some valuable points. When they gave signs of dispersing Anderson would slip out into the street and be selling soap when the gang came along. Twice during the week he went out of town, and, upon his return, talked freely of where he had been, and of his future operations. He had found a good place to sell his stock, and thought of locating permanently, and going into the real estate business. He looked round for a partner, and actually entered into a co-partnership with him, arid bought three houses and lots. This transaction seemed to set at rest the suspicions of Latta, as he paid scarcely any attention afterward to Anderson. When three weeks had passed, the officer had all the points necessary to secure the conviction of the gang, had every one located, and knew at what time he could secure them. He had every day forwarded a report to Lonergan, who advised him as to the steps to be taken. Two or three times Anderson was on the point of raiding by himself, but Lonergan who is well versed in the technicalities of the law, would not permit him to do so as the evidence then in hand was not conclusive enough.

On Last Thursday Anderson had everything fixed to suit him, and telegraphed to Lonergan that things were ready for a pull, and that a big stock of counterfeit money was coming. Lonergan replied that he would be down the next day with John Egan, of St Louis, and make a general raid. On his 'way he called upon Sheriff Pember of Janesville, and the United States Marshal of Wisconsin, and they accompanied him, Anderson had, in the meantime, notified Sheriff Wood, of Green County, who promised to do all in his power to effect the capture of the gang. Lonergan and those with him did not come into Monroe by the cars, as Latta's men know them, but jumped off at a station a few miles off and drove into the place after dark. A meeting was held in Sheriff Wood's office, and a mode of procedure agreed upon. Wood was to post men at roads leading one of town, with instructions to prevent any one leaving; Lonergan and Egan were to start for a house several miles in the country where some plates were supposed to be concealed; while Anderson, the Marshal, and Sheriff Wood were to call at the houses of the members of the gang then at home, five in all, and quietly secure and handcuff them. At 1 o'clock on Saturday morning Henderson's party started out, Lonergan and Egan having been gone on their errand about an hour and a half.

The first house visited was Latta's, which is situated among a copse of woods on the river bank. Anderson knocked on the door, and Latta, who was expecting a large amount of counterfeit money that night, came; but as soon as he saw Anderson, he slammed the door. He was told to open it, or it would be kicked in. He opened it, and before he could make any resistance, was down on the floor and handcuffed. The rooms were searched, as it was known that two others of the clan, Charley Vaughan and Clayton Robinson, slept there. They could not be found, and the officers thought they had slipped away. Seeing a barn in the back part of the yard, Anderson was soon looking into it for the missing men. He found them in the hay-mow, and handcuffed them. Returning to the house with them a general search was made for counterfeit money and tools. A large number of notes, representing about $10,000, on the Brownsville Bank, were found, as were a large number of letters. Several were from a private detective in Chicago, who was acting it would seem, as adviser, not only as to the movements of the government detectives, but as to the disposition of "coney." Some of the letters referred to the hoop-pole business in this way: "Please send me hop-poles twenty feet long; am willing to pay twenty eight cents for them; send me hop-poles ten feet long; if you, have any hop-poles two feet long, send them along". In plain English, hop-poles meant bills; the length given, their denomination; and the price mentioned, the sum in what would be paid per dollar. As soon as the inhabitants of the town appeared upon the streets the fact of the arrests was made known, and fully five hundred people followed the officers and prisoners to the depot, where they were to take the cars for Janesville. The men captured are the ringleaders of the gang. About a dozen of the citizens of Monroe were connected with them, two or three being prominent business men. It was not considered expedient to arrest them as they can be secured at almost any time. They will probably be used as witnesses.

The officers and prisoners arrived safely in Janesville,

and on Saturday morning took Latta and his associates before a United States Commissioner for a hearing. Latta waived the examination, and was held in $15,000 bail for trial. Sherman, Vaughan, and Cole were each in $2,000; and Robinson in $1,000. All were committed to jail in default, and they will be tried at the next session of the United States District court.

The other members of the gang, who are located in different parts of the states mentioned above, are under surveillance, and before this week is out will be in custody. Lonergan, who, as stated, went into the country, was not successful in his mission, the plates having been removed. In a day or two the place where the manufacturing of the notes was carried on will be in the hands of the detective, and it is expected that a number of the plates and a large amount of illegal notes will be found there. The notes circulated by "Bonelatta" and his associates were principally tens, on the Poughkeepsie National Bank. They also dealt extensively in National Twenties and McCartney's (old United States bills) fives and tens. The gang has flooded the entire West with counterfeit money, and their capture entitles Chief Lonergan and Detective Anderson and those that assisted them to the thanks of every law-abiding citizen.

Note: The Latta criminal trial lasted for some time, and eventually culminated in a hung jury.

10

STANLEY EDWARD LATHROP, UNSUNG HERO

Just ten short years after the Mayflower set sail for America seeking religious freedom, the Reverend John Lathrop of England was thrown into prison for preaching his puritan views. After three years in prison, the good Reverend was released. He formed a group of followers and, in 1634, he and 42 of his flock also sailed for America. This was the beginning for the Lathrop name in America.

Moving forward in time to 1776 we find England and America in conflict. Although the Good Reverend John Lathrop had long since made his way to Heaven, you can bet he was up there smiling. For it was his great-great-great grandson, and name sake, the Reverend John Lathrop giving the English a jab in the side. He was the minister of the *Old North Church* in Boston. And as minister, he certainly must have given his permission to use the bell tower as a beacon—*"One if by land, two if by sea."* The Lathrops went on to influence America in many ways. Six former US Presidents had Lathrop blood. A Lathrop served on the Supreme Court. And as you will see, a Nineteenth Century member of the Lathrop clan made a very profound and lasting impact on American society.

Stanley Lathrop was born May 7, 1843 in Orville, New York. He was the son of Congregational minister Alfred Crafts Lathrop. Alfred Lathrop was eight generations apart from the Reverend that came from England, but he shared the same love of God and puritan views of his forefathers. These views were passed on to young Stanley.

Stanley was just ten years old when the Lathrop's moved from New York to the wilderness of Wisconsin, coming first by steamer to Sheboygan, and then by stagecoach to Neenah, where they stayed one year before finally settling in New London. It was here that Reverend Lathrop spent many years preaching the Congregational ways, including abolition, at numerous churches throughout the area.

It was here that young Stanley grew up. At age thirteen, Stanley went to work at the local newspaper office, where he learned a trade that he used throughout much of the rest of his life. He was the "Printer's Devil." At that time, print type consisted of individual letters and numbers carved on wooden blocks. Once the editor wrote the stories, it was the Printer's Devil's job to arrange the blocks on the press for the pages to be printed. Stanley excelled at his job, just as he did in school and in his religious studies. Stanley went on to study at Ripon College, and then Beloit College to become a minister, following in this father's footsteps. It was there at Beloit College that his story really begins. The Civil War broke out in 1861 and the call went out for soldiers for the Union Army. Young men were enlisting all around Stanley. By the following letter he penned to his father, it is quite evident that he, too, was willing and eager to fight for his Country.

Beloit College, April 21, 1861.

Dear Father:

I write to obtain your consent to enlist, as I am not yet eighteen years of age. Since I wrote you, some stirring events have transpired in this country. A few days ago, Fort Sumpter [sic] was in possession of the Federal government, and the glorious old stars and stripes were proudly floating over its battlements. Now it stands a blackened ruin, made so by the traitorous guns of the Southern Confederacy. This is the finishing stroke to a long catalogue of injuries and insults. It is now reported that these rebels are marching upon our national capital, with the professed purpose to wrest the government from our hands, and in its place set up one whose root and foundation is that abomination of abominations, Slavery! It is not enough to make every free man and lover of liberty spring to arms, and to make every drop of blood in our throbbing hearts swell with indignation? When we see the glorious flag of our Union, and the same old banner under which our ancestors fought and bled, torn ignominiously from its place, trampled in the dust, and supplanted by the detestable rattlesnake flag of South Carolina, it is enough to make every patriot gird on the "sword of the Lord and of Gideon," and go willingly to fight the battles of his country and his God. This is why I wish to go and give my services to my country; for, as President Chapin said the other night, to the volunteers in Beloit, "We know that our country is right." I believe that the "irrepressible conflict" between right and wrong, truth and error, freedom and slavery, has come, and I want to help on the side of truth.

I never in my life saw anything like the excitement and enthusiasm which appeared here at the reception of President Lincoln's proclamation calling for 75,000 men. The days of '76 are again revived. There are no democrats or republicans here now - nothing but patriots. Men who but a few days ago were engaged in the bitterest political disputes, are now as a band of brothers, doing all that in them lies for the cause of their country. There was a union meeting held in

Hackett Hall on Wednesday night which was attended by hundreds. Democrats and republicans, students and merchants, ministers and laymen, made patriotic speeches. Among the best speakers were Dr. Brinsmade, pastor of the First Congregational church, Mr. Graves, pastor of the Second Congregational church, and others. The enthusiasm was thrilling. A paper being opened for the names of volunteers, seventeen of the best young men of the town came forward and signed, among whom were some of our most earnest Christian students. The meeting was adjourned till Friday evening. Speeches were made at that time by President Chapin, Senator Bennett, and others of our most distinguished men. Several students spoke, offering themselves as volunteers, amid the wildest excitement. State Senator Bennett said the legislature had just adjourned, after having given the governor $200,000 for the war and five times as much if needed. The legislature also had suspended specie payment of the solvent banks in the state until December, passed a bill to exempt from civil process the property of volunteers, another to protect their families, etc. Quite a number of students enlisted that night, besides others. The full number for a company (78 men) is more than secured already. The city will furnish them with arms, ammunition, uniforms, etc. Governor Randall telegraphed that two regiments are already filled, and two or three more will be needed.

The students bought and raised a large flag over Middle college yesterday. Speeches were made by President Chapin, Professors Porter, Kelsey and several students. It is useless trying to study amid such exciting scenes. Nobody can do it. Quite a number of new students lately arrived, and several enlisted as soon as they could. Two ex-army officers here have offered their services in drilling us. We have formed a company of students and shall begin drilling at once. If President Lincoln issues another call for troops, we shall offer our services to Governor Randall, and if accepted, go immediately into service. President Chapin said in his Sunday afternoon lecture, "It may be that the great battle of Armageddon is at hand; and we must be ready, as Christians and as men, to take our places in the struggle." Professor Blaisdell also has made some stirring speeches.

That our dear country may be delivered from slavery and from all its evils, is the prayer of

> Your Affectionate Son,
> Stanley E. Lathrop.

Two days later, on April 23rd, Stanley wrote his father again, this time to say that he could wait no longer and that he had enlisted. They would be marching to Camp Randall in Madison soon. Thus began the 20,000 mile journey of Chaplin Stanley Lathrop and Wisconsin's Iron brigade – the 1ST Calvary, a journey that included no less than 54 enemy engagements and culminated in the capture of Jefferson Davis. Lathrop's war records indicate he was active in 48 engagements. Having been captured twice, and then mustered out of the Calvary for several months due to injuries, must have kept Stanley from being there for every battle.

In the following article from the *Eau Claire Leader*, March 16, 1906, Stanley relates a sampling of his military experiences:

> In 1862 my regiment made a raid into Arkansas, fighting every day and capturing many prisoners. One day we took a little town after a sharp skirmish, and when we had more prisoners than we had men in our regiment. The Colonel deciding to parole the prisoners detailed me and another soldier printer boy to print blank paroles as soon as possible. The local editor had deserted his little printing office and we took possession. With the old fashioned rude materials we printed the needed paroles on a scorching July day. The prisoners gladly signed the

paroles and went gladly on their way rejoicing.

A few days after a small detachment of us were surrounded by a regiment of Texas rangers and after a fight in which we lost three-fourths of our men, a few of us were captured. We were taken to Little Rock and confined sixteen men in one small room. We asked for something to read but this was refused. Then we organized the "Y.J.B.R.C." which being interpreted means "The Yankee Jail Birds Reading Club". We had neither book nor paper to read. But one member was appointed to repeat what he could remember, for example of Robinson Crusoe, the audience listening criticizing and correcting. Next day another would recite from Hamlet, Julius Caesar, or the Shakespearean plays. Then perhaps Scott's Ivanhoe Rob Roy or Midlothian: then Dickens, Thackeray, or other less famous writers. I even did what few printers have ever done, taught the printer's art in prison. Drawing the outline of a type case on the floor with charcoal and marking the boxes, upper and lower case, we borrowed a jack-knife and whittled out wooden type from a piece of bellywood brought by one of our good natured guards who was curious to see what "them Yanks" could do. We whittled out a "printer's stick" from a piece of board. So I taught the rudiments to some of the boys. Three of them after the war became prosperous printers and publishers.

Another newspaper article recounts further experience of this time period:

"You see, it was mid October 1862. I had been taken prisoner of war in Arkansas, paroled and sent to St. Louis from Little Rock on 'Shank's horses'. All Wisconsin paroled prisoners were sent via Mississippi steamer to old Fort Crawford at Prairie Du Chien where some of us were furloughed and sent home I had railroad transportation to Madison, where I decided to make a bee line to my old home in Westfield, 60 miles North. I started northward on foot, carrying knapsack, overcoat and blanket. Weakened by strenuous campaigning, imprisonment, poor food, chills and fever. I made slow progress. And the miles seemed very long. At last I reached Token Creek, ten miles north, utterly exhausted. Having no pay for six months I was penniless. Telling my story to the kindhearted Token Creek landlord of a little tavern, he was very sympathetic – fed me on the (chicken) fat of the land, and put me to bed where I slept most refreshingly. Starting out next morning with the landlord's breakfast and blessing, I resumed the homeward march. I cannot remember the landlord's name, but I heard later that he raised a company and went to war. Traveling in the teeth of a sharp, cold north wind, I trudged on mile after mile, getting a ride for several miles with an old farmer whose son was in the war down south. There was no railroad to Portage then. Late that night I reached Portage, where another patriotic landlord gave me bed and board, refusing my offer to pay him when I arrived home."

At this time, Stanley Lathrop was mustered out of the 1st Cavalry due to weakened state and disability. The discharge was dated January 10, 1863. Eleven months later, fully recovered, he re-enlisted with Wisconsin's 1st Cavalry and remained until July 19, 1865, just after the capture of Jeff Davis. During his army career, he was a war correspondent for several Wisconsin newspapers, and served as a military job printer under General John C. Fremont in Missouri and Arkansas, under Rosenerans, Grant, and Thomas in Tennessee, and under "Uncle Billy Sherman" in Mississippi, Alabama, Georgia and Florida.

After discharge from the Union Army, Lathrop returned to his home state of Wisconsin, re-entered Beloit College and was graduated in 1867. The following fall, he enrolled at the Chicago Theological Seminary.

The year 1870 was quite eventful for Stanley Lathrop: he graduated from the Seminary and was ordained; he married Elizabeth Littlell of Tomah, Wisconsin; he became the minister of a church in Viroqua, Wisconsin, where he stayed for two years. Then, his calling found him as the minister at his father's church in New London.

Six years later, The American Missionary Association sent him as a missionary to Macon, Georgia. They provided him with a church and a school; he was both pastor and principal. He soon learned that no Negro could draw a book from the public library, so, with the help of friends in the North, he secured a printing press and started a little paper called *The Helping Hand*, taking its title from the motto of Edward Everett Hale, "Look up and not down, look out and not in, and lend a hand." He called his newspaper "a little sheet meant to do good," and by the circulation of his paper, on which he did all the composition and press work, he established the first free library for colored people in the whole South, with contributions of books coming from Henry Ward Beecher, Edward Evertt Hale, George W. Cable, Harriett Beecher Stowe, Mark Twain, his old commander, General Wilson, and a number of leading Southerners as Gen. John B. Gordon and Gov. Joe Brown. White people of Macon gave money for the small library building, in the basement of which was established one of the earliest industrial schools for Negroes in the South. In 1928 the library had 6,000 volumes and was still providing service.

Realizing the destitute condition of the freedmen both in poverty and in mentality, Lathrop strove to help them in body, mind, and spirit. He spread good books, magazines and papers far and wide, and clothing for the needy, received from friends all over the country. The humble beginning of industrial education for the Negroes received generous aid from Mr. Stephen Ballard, so that a separate building for this purpose was erected. Pupils were taught how to build houses and earn good wages as mechanics. Lathrop's wife conducted sewing classes for the women, and at times there were three generations from one family learning to sew garments.

Then came four years of service among the mountain whites, where, in a valley in the Cumberland Mountains, Lathrop strove to bring the light of the gospel and of education among a people ignorant and superstitious. None of the adults could read or write, nor could few of the children. A school, Sherwood Academy, had been established for them, but they resented any idea of progress, and there were times when Lathrop's life was in real danger. Ashamed for their lack of clothes suitable for church, he carried the church to them by holding meetings in the little one-room cabins on the mountainside, where the only light was tallow candles and the kerosene lantern he carried. Many an evening he climbed up steep paths, leading his oldest daughter by the hand, crossing deep mountain canyons on a foot log, and at times carrying his daughter in one arm and the lantern in the other, while the water roared below. The little girl was always a sweet singer and was of great assistance in singing the gospel message in those lonely cabins. In this valley another library was founded of 2400 volumes through the agency of *The Helping Hand.* Here again sewing meetings were held by his faithful helpmate, and the daughter would sing to these humble folk.

After several months of lecturing in New England on his work in the South, Lathrop was promoted to the office of State Superintendent of the American Missionary Association in Texas, but after one year of being almost always away from his home which was so dear to him, he resigned and brought his family back to Wisconsin, where he performed missionary work in the northern part of the state, in one place building a parsonage, and also building two new churches in pioneer communities. Here again he distributed books, magazines and papers everywhere, and founded the *North Wisconsin Traveling Library Association* which sent libraries into many isolated communities and lumber camps. One saloon keeper complained because his business was being ruined when the lumbermen stayed in camp on Sunday and read from the books and papers sent to them instead of drinking and gambling in his saloon.

Lathrop became interested in North Wisconsin Academy and eventually became its traveling agent, raising money, books, students, and friends for its support. This academy developed into Northland College of Ashland, Wisconsin.

The academy had a debt of $18,000 and one building, but at a meeting of its friends, when he was receiving a salary of only $700 with a family of six children to support, he made a liberal subscription, causing considerable sacrifice to him and his family. On such sacrifices Northland College was made possible. His little paper was again busy, asking for books and papers and help for the struggling school.

After Ashland, Lathrop went to Madison to become the State Chaplin for the Grand Army of the Republic (G.A.R.), and in 1915 he became the tour guide for the newly built State Capitol, and wrote its guide book in intricate detail.

In his lifetime over 100,000 books and millions of magazines and papers, and innumerable Bibles and Testaments were given in the South and North, spreading cheer and uplift to plantations, country schools, city slums, penitentiaries, convicts, miners, river boatmen, factory hands, veterans of the Union and Confederate homes, mountaineers, lumbermen, boarding houses, and many others. It is a conservative estimate that at one time or another during his ministry as a soldier of the Cross, over 15,000,000 people were supplied with wholesome and inspiring reading.

Stanley Edward Lathrop called Wisconsin his home. He is truly an unsung hero whose labors have gone unnoticed until now. He never had more than a few dollars in his pocket, but it was the fire and conviction in his heart, to serve God, Country, and his fellow man that sets this gentleman apart.

11

WISCONSIN STREET CARS

There was a time when, in the larger Wisconsin cities, street cars operated on railway systems. As populations grew, the need arose for mass-transit. The typical car, drawn by one or two horses, could comfortably accommodate 25-30 passengers.

Col. George H. Walker opened the first street railway to the public in Milwaukee in 1860; by 1882 in that city, three rail companies operated, each in different sections of the metropolis, a combined total of about 40 cars daily.

All the earliest cars were open; in cold weather, the drivers were muffled in buffalo coats, and the floor was covered with hay to add a little passenger "comfort." Only two lanterns on each coach provided light, one at the fare box behind the driver, and one at the rear. It was a one-man operation, the driver taking care of the fare box and the passengers, as well as tending the horses. During daytime hours, each car was propelled with two horses, but during the evening rush, three were used. Drivers earned 13 cents an hour.

The heaviest traffic occurred on Sundays; it was considered in vogue to ride a trolley to Schlitz Park or the beach, where entire families would go to spend the day.

When electrification of the street car systems began in 1890, the horses and cars were replaced by larger, speedier, motor-driven coaches. By then, the railways had been extended to provide service to a much greater area. Eventually, the tree companies merged into one, which also acquired an independent line to Waukesha.

The new company donated one of the old horse cars to the teachers of the Sixth District school who were in the habit of taking their pupils on weekend outings to Waukesha Beach. The retired car was set up on the wilderness beach and was used for many years as a shelter and headquarters for these jaunts.

That oldest remaining horse-drawn Milwaukee street car was given one last commemorative trip on the streets in 1921. It was mounted on wheels and brought back to the city for Milwaukee's Diamond Jubilee parade. However, it was later dismantled, a relic of the past relegated to the oblivion of lost treasures.

The network of street railway lines in La Crosse that remained in service into the mid-twentieth century was the outgrowth of a horse-drawn system that originated in 1879, extending from Third and Main in downtown to Windsor Street on the north side.

In the spring of that year, David Law and Michael Funk

conceived the idea of organizing what was known as the *La Crosse Street Railway Company* for the purpose of providing passenger transportation service between the north and south sides of the city. The principal industry on the north side was lumber, eight or more saw mills being located on that side of the La Crosse River. Many of the north side mill employees lived in the south side; a plank road connected the two sides of the city, but there were no means of public transportation to get them to and from their work.

The announcement that La Crosse would have a street car line was received with general approval, however, construction of a bridge and laying tracks over the La Crosse River came in question. For a time, it appeared as though this objection might block the project. But one Sunday morning a crew of men was put to work on the job and the line was completed before Monday morning, thus avoiding injunction proceedings. The bridge structure remained and was in service for many years. The company constructed a car barn at Mill and Car Streets where its horses and six small cars were housed.

The Street Railway connected the north and south sides; the fare was five cents; it was well patronized right from the start, and in a short time the line on the north side was extended to Logan Street. This extension proved to be profitable, and in 1888 the company decided to again extend the line still farther north. That part of the city had expanded as a result of the *Chicago-Burlington & Northern*

Railway building through La Crosse on its route between Chicago and Minneapolis. The street car line extension accommodated the large number of employees at the Burlington shops and roundhouse.

About the same time, another street car line was organized, known as the *La Crosse City Railway Company.* This system ran south from the Milwaukee Railroad Depot located in downtown La Crosse (Second and Vine Streets) to Gund's Brewery on Mormon Coulee Road, where the car barn was built.

The two lines were operated independently for several years, but eventually consolidated under the name La *Crosse Street Railway Company.* Further expansion provided transportation service south and east from the downtown area, and when the La Crosse Interstate Fair was organized in 1890, the line was extended to the fairgrounds entrance.

With the extensions, more rolling stock was added until the company owned 19 horse cars. Most of them were drawn by a single horse, each one carrying a bell so the approaching street car could be heard. The front platforms were unprotected from the elements; during winter weather, the drivers wore heavy fur coats, and hay on the floor protected against the cold. The cars were lighted with kerosene lamps, but there were no stoves for heat; windows became coated with thick layers of frost, making it necessary for the passengers to scrape a peep hole to see when they were nearing their destination. During daytime operation, cars ran at ten-minute intervals, each making a round trip in about an hour. After 8:00 PM, the number of cars was reduced.

Although the cars were small, seats ordinarily accommodated 30 passengers. On special occasions, however, as many as 50 people crowded into each car. At these times, two horses were used to power the overloaded coaches.

One of the difficulties encountered with horse cars was their jumping off the tracks, which was a common occurrence. So often did it happen that the passengers willingly assisted in getting the car back on the track rather than suffering a long delay in reaching their destination.

The La Crosse Street Railway system was electrified in 1893, beginning with the first cars operating over the north side line, but before winter set in, the entire city system was equipped with electric cars, the electricity generated at the power station at the corner of Third and La Crosse Streets. The first electrified cars were built by combining two of the old horse cars. One of them—known as "Long Annie," was in service for many years, but over all, this experiment proved unworthy, as the old horse cars were too frail to withstand the heavier loads and rougher use to which they were subjected, and that idea was soon abandoned. The old horse cars were relegated to use as trailers during special occasions.

The new *Orange Line* buses that appeared in Janesville July, 1929 caused quite a stir, however, exactly 43 years earlier, more excitement erupted over the new street car line.

The first trip over the street railway in Janesville was made on July 22, 1886, as car No. 1 was placed on the tracks at the railroad crossing on Academy Street at 8:30 AM. Only the company officers and two or three citizens were allowed to board, as the car was only to be run over the road for the purpose of an inspection. After a brief stop near the Commercial Hotel to repair a harness, the car continued on to the "end of the line" at Pearl and Washington Streets. Then it proceeded to the opposite "end of the line" across the Milwaukee Street Bridge to North Main. It attracted considerable attention all along the route; it was, of course, the first street car to appear in the city, and quite a curiosity to many.

The tracks were deemed in very good condition, and the passengers on board were quite pleased with the opportunity to be the first to ride a Janesville street car.

These cars were considerably smaller than those used in the bigger cities, attractively painted white with yellow panels; numbers and the words "Janesville Street Railway" over the windows in silver leaf. The insides were finished in the color of natural maple and ash wood. Glass transoms and ventilators provided an ample supply of fresh air. Five strong, well-built horses were bought for use on the railway, and all were quite capable of taking a loaded car from one end of the line to the other without trouble. However, when the line was extended to the fairgrounds, an extra horse was used for assistance with loaded cars up the steep grade to East Milwaukee Street.

Advancement in the design of motor cars, making them more useable year-round, perhaps was the beginning of the street car decline in Wisconsin in the 1930s. Most were gone by the mid-1900s. But what a grand piece of history they added to Wisconsin's past!

12

THE CLARENCE BRIDGE

On the east bank of the Sugar River about three miles southwest of present-day Brodhead, once was the bustling little village of Clarence. Settled in 1841, it was first known as Tenneyville; brothers A.D. Tenney and B.J. Tenney platted the land, sold lots, and established a small store. The settlement soon had a hotel, blacksmith shop, a steam-powered furniture factory, and the first physician in the area. The post office was established in the Tenney home, and a school district was organized. By 1856, Clarence was a flourishing village, anticipated to become a major metropolis of southwestern Wisconsin. That, of course, did not happen, as the railroad chose the location of Brodhead for its depot, and as with so many bypassed small villages of that time, Clarence sadly withered away.

At first, as there was no bridge spanning the Sugar River, Jacob Ten Eyck, the resident nearest the river, kept a raft on which he ferried the people of the community and travelers. A bridge was finally built, but every year it washed out with the spring floods. Then in early fall of 1864, heavy pilings were driven at each bank, and construction began on a unique span bridge, 130 feet in length with a sixteen feet wide driveway. It was the only one of its kind, built by a Racine, Wisconsin contractor named Hulburt. It was raised on the ice during an exceptionally good season for such a project. But an early spring and high water forced the contractor to rush the finish, cutting away the underpinning before he was completely ready; however, no serious effects resulted.

At that time, covered bridges were not uncommon; within a few years, the Clarence Bridge was enclosed and roofed, but it was never painted. Watchful township supervisors discovered that the tremendously heavy superstructure was slowly settling; the eight inch crown had fallen to five inches. Although the contractor had been paid in full and the work accepted, he returned to reinforce the main framework by spiking in on each side heavy arches made with two thicknesses of two-by-twelve planks, requiring thousands of board-feet of lumber.

The reinforcement arches seemed to be adequate for quite some time, however, it was later evident that the structure was still settling, and another attempt was made to strengthen the bridge with iron suspending rods. It was left this way for several years, but the crown entirely disappeared, leaving a flat floor. About 1907 it was decided to do what should have been done in the beginning. A concrete abutment was built under the bridge in the middle of the river. The end abutments were also reconstructed with concrete, and this made a very stable bridge. Until that time, the Clarence Bridge had been one of the longest single span structures of its kind in Southern Wisconsin.

In its day, the bridge played some sinister roles. Before the turn of the twentieth century, holdups were frequent in the shelter of the bridge; highwaymen would often hide themselves in the timbers of the bridge's roof, and when a likely looking team would drive into the bridge, the thugs would drop from hiding and gather their loot with very desirable privacy. Horse thefts were also common, the robbers using the same techniques as their brothers in crime who sought cash and other valuables.

In later years, the bridge, once again, was part of a criminal act when the police of two states were searching for Fred Hartin, confessed murderer. Hartin had committed the dastardly deed in a little cabin across the Rock River and then came to Beloit, but managed to evade police and fled before he was arrested.

In his flight he reached the covered bridge just ahead of a group of officers. Seeing them approaching, he slipped under the bridge and hid on one of the big beams over the water. The fugitive lay in this lair for the entire night while the officers paced back and forth in the covered span overhead, guarding against Hartin's attempt to use the bridge as a means of escaping to the west. When they finally went to a nearby farmhouse at dawn to use the telephone, Hartin realized his opportunity, and he fled.

A year and a half later, Hartin was captured in the east by operatives of the Diamond Detective Agency. During his confession, he told of how the covered bridge at Clarence had helped him to escape.

The Clarence covered bridge served travelers of southern Wisconsin until 1931. As motorcar and truck traffic increased, the structure was deemed inadequate; regrettably, the old landmark was destroyed when a new bridge was erected to meet the needs of the time.

13

WISCONSIN NATIVES

The territory now known as Wisconsin became home to many Native American tribes long before any European explorers arrived. Although many of these tribe names are familiar to us today as "Wisconsin" tribes, most of them did not originate there, but rather migrated to the region from various other locations. And because these earliest people who populated Wisconsin Territory had no written language to record their migration travels, only the artifacts they left behind are our clues to determine their presence, their cultural traits, and movement patterns. Extensive archaeological studies have uncovered some very surprising facts regarding the presence of human habitation in various Wisconsin areas—some widespread, and some isolated.

A thousand years ago Wisconsin was inhabited mostly by wild creatures. However, there did exist at that time people of an advanced culture. When evidence of their earlier presence in Wisconsin was first discovered in 1836 by a settler at a location about 50 miles west of the new village of Milwaukee, little was known about the long since vanished civilization. But the flat-topped pyramid-like mounds found there were definitely man-made, and soon became a great curiosity and subject of broad study.

The name Aztalan was given to the site of an apparent village by Judge Nathaniel Hyer, an early resident of Milwaukee. Reports of the ruins of an ancient walled city had reached Milwaukee, and from the description, Hyer took great interest in seeing it for himself. He traveled on horseback to the site in 1836, and again in 1837 to draw the first map of the area. His narrative description and map were published in Chicago and Milwaukee newspapers. He compared his observations with reports he had read about the Aztecs in Mexico, who also built similar pyramids of stone. Their traditional lore told of ancestors coming from a land they called Aztalan, a place in the distant north. Hyer jumped to the conclusion that this was that place, and incorrectly named the site Aztalan. At first, his assumption was accepted, and the name remained.

Investigation of this band of people would eventually reveal that they mysteriously abandoned the village and disappeared from Wisconsin about AD 1250. They were of the Mississippian Culture, and are believed to have migrated north to Wisconsin after the last ice sheet had disappeared and had been replaced by vegetation. These people came from Cahokia, another ancient city located across the Mississippi River from present-day St. Louis, Missouri. Aztalan's direct connection with Cahokia is apparent in the likeness of mound construction and cultural traits revealed by thousands of artifacts that have been uncovered.

The site of Aztalan developed into the largest and most significant archaeological survey in the state of Wisconsin. In a century and a half of intense study, the thousands of artifacts recovered from the site have aided in determining Aztalan culture. Professional archaeological excavation has revealed much evidence as to paint a fairly accurate picture of the ancient city, and has helped us to better understand what Aztalan was and who built it.

Increase A. Lapham, considered as Wisconsin's first scientist, also made a study of the Aztalan site and drew more detailed maps of the 21-acre village and its surrounding area in 1850. He, too, concurred with Hyer regarding the similarities with Mexican Aztec "architecture" which led him to believe this was the land of Aztalan, an important segment of Aztec lore.

It would be after the turn of the Twentieth Century when the Wisconsin Archeological Society was formally chartered (1906) and efforts were made to preserve and document the site. By that time, unfortunately, treasure seekers had severely damaged the mounds digging for relics, and farmers had plowed and planted crops on the land, all but leveling many of the visible features. Fortunately, Lapham's maps had recorded them.

The myths of Aztalan's connection to the Mexican Aztecs were finally disproved. Attention was then appropriately directed to the association with the Mississippian Culture of Cahokia in Illinois.

A population of some 500 people made their homes within the walled city of Aztalan. The fortification walls surrounding the settlement were constructed of vertical timbers and then plastered with a clay and grass mixture to give the appearance of concrete. Houses were built in the same manor using thatched or bark roofs. Archaeologists have determined that the large flat-topped mounds weren't necessarily burial mounds as have been discovered elsewhere, but were built for the purpose of conducting rituals, and perhaps to place the houses of important people of the town, namely a chief and his family. Inside the enclosure, too, was a large plaza for social activities, housing sectors for the common citizens, and large underground food storage facilities. Without any doubt, this civilization was well organized and structured. Although the Mississippian culture did not have a written language, their history and lifestyle has been pieced together through artwork left behind in the form of pottery and crafts, tools, implements, and weaponry.

Outside the fortification walls, vast fields of corn were cultivated by the Mississippian farmers. In addition they grew squash, pumpkins and sunflowers. It is safe to say that Aztalan was the first farming town in Wisconsin, hundreds of years before Europeans set foot on the soil. They were probably attracted to this region along the banks of the Crawfish River because of its abundant fish and clam, wild game, (especially deer) large flocks of waterfowl, and dense stands of wild rice. The setting was perfect with ample resources to support their population.

From the remains that have been found and studied, it is known that fire destroyed the city, but it is not certain what caused the disaster. There is some speculation that the people of Aztalan practiced cannibalism to some degree, and it is quite possible that other Indian tribes intentionally burned the town and drove its occupants away.

In more recent times, a number of various native cultures occupied various parts of Wisconsin, but as mentioned earlier, most origins were not Wisconsin. Many came from the North American eastern seaboard; their migration to the Midwest resulted from several reasons: climate surely was a factor in some cases; depletion of food sources in their home areas caused some to seek new hunting grounds; the intrusion of Europeans drove some westward; and what seems to be the most dramatic factor was the hostile attitudes of some tribes toward others.

Of all the Native tribes that have lived in Wisconsin, only the Menominee and the Winnebago were true aboriginals whose existence in the region extends beyond human memory, possibly 5000 years. The Winnebago do not remember a time when they didn't live at Red Banks on the south shore of Green Bay. Their occupation of Wisconsin is very ancient; although they have no recollection of mound-building, they may very well be descendents of the earlier Mississippian, Hopewell, and Adena cultures. Their original homeland was the northeast Wisconsin area between Green Bay and Lake Winnebago, but they eventually dominated most of Wisconsin from Upper Michigan to present-day Milwaukee, and west to the Mississippi River.

The Menominee's earliest known homeland was near Sault Ste. Marie and Michilimackinac. Sometime around 1400 they were forced southwest by the arrival of the Ojibwe and Potawatomi from the east. Their new homeland was along the Menominee River, present-day border between Wisconsin and Upper Michigan. Their territory extended north to Escanaba, Michigan, and south to Oconto, Wisconsin prior to the arrival of the French fur traders. Becoming quite active in the fur trade, they quickly extended their hunting region west. By 1700, the once dominating Winnebago had nearly been wiped out by war and epidemic, and the Menominee spread south and west, occupying the vacated space. At their peak, the Menominee controlled most of central Wisconsin. However, after 1832, white settlement and commercial logging rapidly reduced their available land and were eventually confined to a 235,000 acre reservation in northeast Wisconsin, where they have remained to present day.

The first Frenchman to encounter the two friendly tribes was Jean Nicollet in 1634 and again in 1639. But during the next 30 years, the relatively peaceful conditions in northern Wisconsin were disrupted. Thousands of refugees—Potawatomi, Fox, Sauk, Ottawa, Huron, Mascouten, Kickapoo, Tionontati—had been maliciously forced from their homelands in the eastern Great Lakes regions by the formidable, warring Iroquois of New York. As they fled west to avoid massacre, they relocated in northern Wisconsin and Upper Michigan. The same pressure drove the Ojibwe south and west from Sault Ste. Marie.

This enormous and sudden influx nearly destroyed the aboriginal Winnebago and Menominee. Competition for available resources had transformed Wisconsin into a place of war, epidemic, and starvation. The Sturgeon War between the Menominee and Ojibwe resulted as the Menominee placed a series of fences across the Menominee River to easily catch the sturgeon swimming upstream from Lake Michigan to spawn. The restrictions prevented any of the fish from getting into the Ojibwe territory, cutting off the much needed food supply. Warnings from the Ojibwe were ignored, and the Ojibwe attacked and destroyed a Menominee village. Because they were too few in number, the Menominee were unable to retaliate alone, so they sought assistance from the Fox, Sauk, and Potawatomi near Green Bay, thus spreading the conflict far beyond the original opponents. At the same time, the unrelenting Iroquois warriors had pursued the fleeing eastern tribes to Michigan and Wisconsin, and were attacking and destroying anyone they encountered.

The hostile conditions in Wisconsin had resulted from a series of events long before that occurred far to the east. Knowing the warring nature of the Iroquois, the French had suppressed trade relations with them, avoiding their acquisition of firearms, but had supplied the Algonquin and Montagnais with weapons. These tribes were then able to drive the Iroquois from the St. Lawrence Valley in 1610. The Dutch, however, were more interested in the profits of trade than in keeping peace, and the Iroquois soon entered into trade relations with the Dutch along the Hudson River. By 1645 the Iroquois had taken control of the lower Ottawa Valley, blocked access to the western Great Lakes, and brought the French fur trade to a halt. With so few Frenchmen in North America at the time, they had no choice but to make peace with the Iroquois, forcing them to remain neutral while the Iroquois attacked and destroyed the Huron in 1649. Within the next three years, other French allies suffered a similar fate.

For a few years, the French maintained the truce with the Iroquois, and encouraged what remained of their allies to deliver furs to Montreal. The Ottawa, Huron and Ojibwe formed large canoe fleets to force their way past Iroquois war parties on the Ottawa River. The Iroquois retaliated by attacking the refugee villages in Wisconsin.

Encouraged immigration had greatly increased French population in Canada; now they were better able to resist the Iroquois aggression and soon ended the peace agreement. A regiment of French soldiers began a series of attacks on villages in the Iroquois homeland in 1664. The French then resumed travel and trade in the western Great Lakes region.

A year later, fur trader Nicolas Perrot, Jesuit Claude-Jean Allouez, and other Frenchmen accompanied a large Huron and Ottawa trading party on its return journey from Montreal. They fought their way past the Ottawa Valley Iroquois and arrived at Green Bay just at the approach of winter; this was the first French appearance in the area since Nicolet in 1634. But there had been a drastic population reduction in the original Wisconsin tribes. The Menominee and Winnebago had nearly been exterminated, with less than 400 Menominee and only a remnant of the once dominant Winnebago remaining. War and epidemic had created the chaotic conditions that lingered until 1667 when the French finally gained the upper hand on the Iroquois.

The peace lasted thirteen years, allowing the French to resume their fur trade, and to bring stability to the region. Perrot established a trading post at Green Bay, and missionaries followed a couple of years later. Although the Jesuits visited the Menominee, most of their efforts were concentrated on the Huron and Ottawa, with whom they had enjoyed some earlier successful converts. The Menominee kept their traditional religion for the time being, but trade was another issue, as the Menominee underwent a fundamental economic change and became hunters for profit. Competition for hunting territory might have added to an already tense situation, but the French used their influence to terminate much of the warfare; it interfered with the fur trade. Nicolas Perrot understood native peoples well and began to mediate the intertribal disputes near Green Bay, benefitting all parties and allowing the French trade to expand.

Although the French fur trade caused much of their troubles, it also saved the Menominee and Winnebago from extinction by restricting warfare and mediating the disputes, but some serious problems remained. Perrot was able to reconcile a Fox-Ojibwe war, and Daniel Dulhut arranged a peace between the Ojibwe and Dakota, there was still friction in the region due to crowding which the French could never resolve completely. They never achieved a satisfactory relationship with the Fox, and the ever-present hostility between the Ojibwe and Dakota periodically erupted into confrontations for hunting territory along the southern shore of Lake Superior.

The peace in the western Great Lakes region came to a violent end in 1680 with yet another Iroquois attack against the Illinois. However, the unity that had evolved during the period of peace prevailed; the Iroquois could no longer have their way in the west without serious opposition.

The Iroquois failure to conquer Fort St. Louis on the upper Illinois River in 1684 was the turning point in the Beaver Wars. The French began to organize and arm the Algonquin. Taking the offensive in 1687, the alliance had to Iroquois on the run back towards New York. The war finally concluded with a peace treaty signed in 1701, leaving the French and their allies in control of the Great Lakes. Unfortunately, the timing of this victory coincided with an overabundance of beaver fur on the European market. Prices dropped sharply. In addition, Jesuit protest about the corruption that the fur trade had created among Native Americans influenced the decision by the French crown to suspend fur trade in the western Great Lakes region. The trading post at Green Bay closed, taking the Menominee temporarily out of the fur trade.

The defeated Iroquois were quick to take advantage of the opportunity to weaken the French by offering their native allies access to the British traders at Albany. As a rule, British goods were of better quality and at a lower price. The ploy was a success, and the French alliance soon fell apart. In desperation, the French in Canada convinced Paris to permit the establishment of a new post at Detroit for trade with the Great Lakes tribes in 1701. Virtually every tribe moved to the vicinity of the new post, with the exception of the Menominee and Winnebago who remained in Wisconsin. Their small population had played no part in the French and Algonquin victory over the Iroquois, and they were too far west for the offers of British trade goods.

They had no intentions of leaving their homeland to settle near Fort Pontchartrain at Detroit.

This turn of events was beneficial to the Menominee; the refugee tribes began leaving northern Wisconsin. Relations with the Dakota and Ojibwe remained friendly, and they could once again hunt, fish, and gather wild rice with a certain amount of peace and security. Slowly, the Menominee population began to recover.

Tension at Fort Pontchartrain caused by overcrowding by too many tribes resulted in conflict; the French were attacked by Fox, Mascouten, and Kickapoo. Other French allies rushed in to assist; a great slaughter followed, and the Fox and their allies were forced back to Wisconsin where they continued to attack the French and their allies.

The Fox Wars were civil wars between members of the Great Lakes alliance, and they must have been certain satisfaction to the Iroquois and British. The Menominee remained neutral during the first Fox War. Fighting ended in 1716, but the Fox continued to antagonize the French with their constant confrontations with the Illinois and Osage. As the Fox acquired other native allies to fight these enemies, the French began to suspect a threat, and decided to destroy the Fox. They isolated the Fox from potential allies, and after convincing the Winnebago and Dakota to switch sides, they attacked the Fox in 1728. This time, the Menominee were involved; they refused Fox alliance and joined the French. A combined Winnebago, Menominee, Ojibwe war party attacked a Fox hunting village, killing at least 80 warriors and capturing some 70 women and children.

Meanwhile, the French had reoccupied their old fort at Green Bay. Concerned about possible retaliation from the Fox, the Winnebago moved closer to Green Bay and built a fortified village on an island in the Fox River. Their enemy soon found them, but the fortification was too strong for an effective attack, so they waited for an opportunity.

At Green Bay, the French commander heard of the battle and set out with French militia and Menominee warriors. The Fox finally abandoned the siege.

This second Fox War turned even uglier when, in 1730, most of the Fox decided to flee east to join the Iroquois. But the French and their allies caught up with them in northern Illinois. During that battle, the Fox were almost annihilated; a few survivors found refuge with the Sauk near Green Bay. A French expedition followed them to the village and demanded their surrender. When the Sauk refused, another battle ensued, and the French commander was killed. As the French retreated to regroup, the Sauk and Fox took this opportunity to abandon their village and fled west. They crossed the Mississippi River and settled in Iowa. The following year, another French expedition, accompanied by Menominee warriors, was sent there to seek and destroy the Sauk and Fox in their new refuge. This effort also failed.

By this time, the French allies were becoming alarmed with the idea of genocide. At a conference in Montreal, the

Menominee and Winnebago asked the French to show mercy to the Fox, while the Potawatomi and Ottawa made the same request on behalf of the Sauk. Because they were confronted by new conflicts with the Dakota in the west and the Chickasaw in the south, the French reluctantly agreed to a peace with the Fox and Sauk. Despite their efforts to stop the French from completely destroying them, the Fox and Sauk never forgave the Menominee for their participation in the second Fox War; a lasting hostility had been created.

The Menominee, though, were at peace with almost every other tribe in the region. Following the Fox Wars, their alliance with the French was even stronger. Their numbers had increased while the population of others had fallen, and they began to expand southwestward into central Wisconsin areas recently vacated by the Sauk and Fox. Although the neighboring Ojibwe and Dakota were bitter enemies to each other, neither tribe objected to the Menominee movement. The Menominee maintained friendly relations with both; they could hunt freely in territory where Dakota and Ojibwe warriors would kill each other when they met. Only the Fox and Sauk remained a threat.

The Menominee and Winnebago joined with other tribes to aid the French in protecting Quebec from British invasion, although the Menominee contribution to the war effort was minimal. They were also involved in other conflicts, allied with Ojibwe, Potawatomi and Mascouten against the Peoria in1746, and with the Winnebago in a separate war west of the Mississippi River against the Missouri. The pattern of limited participation by the Menominee continued in the last major conflict between Britain and France for the control of North America—the French and Indian War of 1755-63. But that participation came at a price: while fighting in the east, the Great Lakes warriors contracted smallpox in 1757 and brought it back to their homeland villages that winter. The resulting epidemic left the Menominee with only 800 people, and combined with fewer trade goods put a strain on their French loyalty. As the war turned against them, the French grew arrogant and abusive, and a Menominee uprising at Green Bay killed 22 French soldiers. The Menominee soon regretted their actions, as members of the war party were later captured and sent to Montreal for punishment; several were executed.

But the capture of Quebec by the British ended the French reign in North America. Montreal surrendered the next year, and by 1761, British soldiers occupied Green Bay. The breakdown of French authority in the region had brought the Winnebago, Menominee, and Potawatomi at Green Bay to the verge of war with the Michilimackinac Ojibwe, but the British assumed the old French practice of mediating and providing trade goods. Preventing the outbreak of serious warfare, the British won the trust and loyalty of the Winnebago and Menominee. During the next 50 years, the Winnebago and Menominee would ally with the British, fighting both the Spanish and Americans during the Revolutionary War and the War of 1812.

After the War of 1812, settlement began to advance up the Mississippi from St. Louis, but warfare in Iowa and Minnesota between the Dakota, Ojibwe, Fox, and Sauk slowed its progress. The government attempted to end the fighting in 1825 at a grand council held with the area's tribes at Prairie du Chien. Attended by the Ojibwe, Fox, Sauk, Menominee, Iowa, Sioux, Winnebago, Ottawa, and Potawatomi, the resulting treaty established boundaries between them. It also created a 40-mile wide buffer zone between the Dakota, Fox and Sauk in northeast Iowa. Called the Neutral Ground, the Americans hoped to relocate the Winnebago there since they were friendly with both sides, but the Winnebago did not favor this arrangement. Since its purpose was to smooth the progress of settlement, the treaty made almost no provisions to protect native lands from white encroachment. It had only little success in preventing warfare, but settlement afterwards moved northward at an accelerated pace. During the next fifteen years, the Winnebago were forced to surrender most of their homeland. Miners rushed in to claim the rich lead deposits in northwestern Illinois and southwestern Wisconsin, and nothing was done by the government to prevent encroachment. Less than two years after a treaty was signed at Prairie du Chien, the Winnebago declared war to defend their territory. Led by the Winnebago Prophet White Cloud and the war chief Red Bird, fighting began in the summer of 1827 when a barge ascending the Mississippi near Prairie du Chien was fired upon. Other attacks killed some settlers along the lower Wisconsin River and struck the lead mines near Galena, Illinois. Soldiers were rushed north from St. Louis, and by August it was over. Faced with a war they could not win, Red Bird and White Cloud surrendered. Red Bird died in prison, but White Cloud was pardoned by the president and was released. Meanwhile, in a treaty signed at Green Bay in August, 1828, the Winnebago, Ojibwe, Potawatomi, and Ottawa ceded northern Illinois for $540,000.

The last serious conflict between Americans and the natives in Wisconsin came in 1832. Blackhawk's Sauk tribe at Rock Island, Illinois refused to relinquish their land, but after the Menominee and Dakota murdered fifteen Fox chiefs enroute to a meeting with the Americans at Prairie du Chien, war seemed eminent. Blackhawk brought his people west into Iowa to protect the Fox and Sauk villages there from the Dakota attacks which never came. When he started back to Illinois, the Americans refused to allow him to cross the Mississippi.

In the spring of 1832, the chief defiantly led his people back across the Mississippi to reclaim their former territory, convinced that the British and other native tribes would join him against the Americans. This was the first act that touched off the Blackhawk War. The anticipated help did not materialize; pursued by the army and Illinois militia, Blackhawk retreated towards Wisconsin hoping to reach safety among either the Winnebago or Ojibwe. But most

Winnebago wanted nothing to do with him and refused to help. After several confrontations, Blackhawk realized that he no longer had friends among the other native tribes. He turned his people westward in an attempt to return to Iowa, but they never made it. Trapped between an American army and gunboat at the mouth of the Bad Axe River, the Sauk were slaughtered before surrendering. Menominee and Dakota warriors killed many of those who managed to elude capture by the Americans.

Chief Blackhawk, however, escaped before the battle and fled north. He was captured by the Winnebago Chief Choukeka, a friend of the Americans, who delivered him to the Indian Agent at Prairie du Chien.

The Winnebago ceded their land east of the Mississippi in a harsh treaty negotiated by General Winfield Scott at Fort Armstrong in September, 1832, and agreed to move to Neutral Ground in northeast Iowa. Over the next four decades they were moved and removed many times to locations in Minnesota, South Dakota, and Nebraska. Some had managed to stay in Wisconsin, but were routinely being arrested and transported to the Nebraska reservation. Within a month, they were usually back in Wisconsin. After ten years of this game, the government finally gave up and purchased homestead lands for the Winnebago, and let them stay. During the 1880s, over half of the Nebraska Winnebago came home to Wisconsin where they have remained every since, scattered across ten counties.

As for the Menominee, a final treaty signed with the

United States in 1856 ceded two townships for the purpose of creating a reservation. This reservation included 235,000 acres of their homeland. Joined later by a small group of Potawatomi, the Menominee have remained in this location ever since. But it wasn't always as easy as it sounds; timber interests in northern Wisconsin became the focal point of wealth seekers, and it was soon observed that the government had made an error by giving this valuable White Pine timberland to the Menominee. Every known dishonest means was attempted to relieve the tribe of the 350 square miles of prime forest, but all efforts failed. Under government supervision, the Menominee began operation of their own tribally-owned and operated sawmill in 1872 which competed with all other private lumber companies in the area. Wisconsin's timber was soon depleted, and the many lumber barons moved on, but the Menominee remained. They began a program of sustained yield harvest in 1908, the first large scale application of this concept in the United States. Designed to assure an income for future generations, it was a great success, and the lumber industry remained the primary source of income for the Menominee.

The Federal Government terminated the Menominee's tribal status in 1961, and their reservation became a Wisconsin county. The sawmill could no longer provide enough tax base to pay for all the services a county government was required to provide, and the Menominee instantly went from being one of the most self-sufficient tribes in the United States to the lowest standard of living in Wisconsin. To meet their obligations, the Menominee were forced to sell part of their reservation as lakefront lots for vacation homes. Federal recognition was restored in 1973.

14

SHULLSBURG UNDER SIEGE

Green Bay on the western shore of Lake Michigan and Prairie du Chien on the eastern bank of the Mississippi River are well-known as being the two oldest cities in Wisconsin, established as a result of the earliest exploration to the Wisconsin Territory. They were the primary trading posts during the early fur trading era, and important military installations were located there as well.

But what of the *third* oldest city in Wisconsin? Seldom remembered in that light, Shullsburg in Southwest Wisconsin has that distinction. The surrounding area was the first part of the state to be permanently settled as Americans from the East and emigrants—mostly from Ireland and England—arrived to engage in mining of lead, an industry that brought great wealth to Wisconsin.

Galena, in Northwest Illinois was already a well-established mining and trade center, with access to the Mississippi River via the Fever River. In time, Galena would become a busy steamboat port, shipping huge quantities of lead mined in Northwest Illinois and Southwest Wisconsin. An agent of John Jacob Astor's American Fur Company was sent to the area in the summer of 1819. Young Jesse Shull built a trading house at Galena, and began exploring the surrounding region in search for additional locations. Although his primary concern was for the interests of the fur trading company, he had also acquired a personal interest in mining. Following Indian trails northward, he entered into Wisconsin Territory where, in 1820, he made his first camp at the site of present-day Shullsburg. For several years he maintained a good rapport with the Indians for trading purposes; they eventually led him to locations of rich ore deposits.

By then, Galena had grown to the extent that there was little room for newcomers; available mining claims in the area were becoming scarce. Waves of miners migrated northward, and many new settlements established as miners found "new diggins'"... among them, New Dublin, where Jesse Shull had set up his trading post. Some of these early settlements still remain today as active cities and villages: Hazel Green was first known as Hardscrabble; Benton was originally Cottonwood Hill; New Dublin was renamed Shullsburg. Some of the towns did not survive after the miners migrated west during the Gold Rush days: little or no remaining signs that they ever existed are left at Gratiot's Grove, Veta Grand, Natchez, Buncombe, and Etna.

Shullsburg grew and prospered until the Civil War,

lead mining its principal economic factor. But when the mining played out, unlike many other mining towns that withered and died, Shullsburg managed to survive and remained a thriving community.

And this is where our story begins, in the early morning hours of June 25, 1925.

It was sometime past midnight when five armed men boldly rode into Shullsburg driving a high powered car. At the edge of town, they secretly cut the phone lines that connected the community with the rest of the world. Their plan was to rob the First National Bank. The whole town was asleep, so the robbers had no intentions of making this a hurried operation, nor were they concerned about silently sneaking about in the shadows. Their leader, dressed in a policeman's cap and a long, belted overcoat, stood on a corner of Water Street—the main thoroughfare through the business district—and directed operations with the "coolness of a traffic cop."

"Take your time. No hurry... the town's asleep," he told his comrades. And they did take their time—over two hours.

Two of the gang broke through the front doors of the bank; the others remained on the street outside as sentinels to thwart any interference. Inside, the two destroyed the bank's fire alarm, and then proceeded to set off a charge of nitroglycerin to blow up the vault. But the blast did more than wreck the vault; the large plate glass windows at the front shattered, as well as the rest of the windows on the side and rear of the building. All the furniture was demolished, the remains of busted lighting fixtures scattered everywhere, and gaping holes were left in the ceiling.

The noise from the explosion naturally drew some attention, but the gunmen on the street kept everyone at bay; the night telephone operator was threatened... told to stay in the office or she could be killed. A man in a nearby hotel leaned from his window to get a better look at what was going on, but one of the gang on the street spotted him and fired a shot, just missing the man and putting a hole in the hotel sign. Approaching motorists—a traveling salesman and another tourist—were ordered to stop. When they didn't, their headlights were shot out and tires flattened. The entire town was under siege.

Loot gathered and secure, the bandits fled in their powerful car, their identities unknown.

With the phone lines disabled, there was no way to quickly summon help, or to warn neighboring cities of impending danger. When it seemed safe, residents of Shullsburg drove the ten miles to Scales Mound in Illinois to sound the alarm. But the fugitives were long gone; they had escaped and disappeared as mysteriously as they had arrived several hours earlier.

The chaos in Shullsburg, however, was not over. All day, hoards of people swarmed about, trying to get a glimpse of the wrecked bank interior while workmen boarded up the front, side and rear windows. The bank opened at 9:00 o'clock, and patrons were informed that within a day or two, it would be business as usual. But the town was still trembling over the excitement of the early morning disaster; townspeople and visitors continued to crowd around the bank until late evening to find out what had happened.

First National Bank president, James Simpson told news reporters that the loss was large, but because of the state of confusion in the aftermath of such an event, it would be difficult to determine the exact amount of money stolen. Bank officers would have to examine the books. First estimations were $75,000. However, after some initial investigation, the amount was thought to be much lower.

A milkman on his way home from making a delivery stopped to pick raspberries near Lena, Illinois—a mere 30 miles from Shullsburg—where he discovered a sugar sack that had been discarded along the roadway. Upon examination of the sack, he found papers, bank notes, and other items belonging to the First National Bank at Shullsburg. He notified the bank of his find, and although the contents were of no value to anyone except the bank, the evidence did point authorities in the direction of the thieves' escape route.

Five suspects were captured and arrested on October 20, 1925 in and near Bloomington, Illinois: James Ford, John Adams, John Thompson, Thomas Foster, and Joe Dawale, AKA "Chicago Blackie" were brought to the Lafayette

County Jail in Darlington, Wisconsin, and were held under a $100,000 bond each.

The amount of money stolen had been determined to be $25,000. The prosecutor and special agents who worked on the case were confident of a conviction. At the conclusion of the trial, the jury was out for ten hours. When they returned and the clerk read their verdict, everyone was astounded upon hearing that the five men had been found not guilty on grounds that there wasn't enough evidence for a conviction.

Immediately following the verdict, Dawale and Thomas were re-arrested by deputy sheriffs from Carlyle, Illinois, wanted there in connection with another recent bank robbery. Foster was also arrested on an unrelated charge. Adams and Ford were set free.

Five other men were later arrested in Central Illinois for a different bank robbery. They were said to be seen in Shullsburg a day prior to the First National Bank incident. Perhaps the Shullsburg bank robbers finally got their just reward.

ABOUT THE AUTHOR

J.L. Fredrick lived his youth in rural Western Wisconsin, a modest but comfortable life not far from the Mississippi River. His father was a farmer, and his mother, an elementary school teacher. He attended a one-room country school for his first seven years of education.

Wisconsin has been home all his life, with exception of a few years in Minnesota and Florida. After college in La Crosse, Wisconsin and a stint with Uncle Sam during the Viet Nam era, the next few years were unsettled as he explored and experimented with life's options. He entered into the transportation industry in 1975 where he remained until retirement in 2012. He is a long-time member of the Wisconsin State Historical Society.

Since 2001 he has fourteen published novels to his credit, and two non-fiction history volumes, *Rivers, Roads, & Rails,* and *Ghostville.* He was a featured author during Grand Excursion 2004.

J.L. Fredrick is currently exploring the U.S. in an RV.

www.ingramcontent.com/pod-product-compliance
Lightning Source LLC
Chambersburg PA
CBHW062227080426
42734CB00010B/2057